Using Video to Support Teacher Reflection and Development in ELT

Reflective Practice in Language Education
Series Editor: Thomas S. C. Farrell, Brock University

This series covers different issues related to reflective practice in language education and includes an introductory book which introduces these areas. The other books in the series clarify the different approaches that have been taken within reflective practice and outline current themes that have emerged in the research on various topics and methods of reflection that have occurred.

Published:

Reflective Practice in ELT
Thomas S. C. Farrell

Cooperative Learning through a Reflective Lens
George M. Jacobs, Anita Lie and Siti Mina Tamah

Micro-Reflection on Classroom Communication: A FAB Framework
Hansun Zhang Waring and Sarah Chepkirui Creider

Reflecting on Leadership in Language Education
Edited by Andy Curtis

Forthcoming:

English Language Teacher Beliefs
Farahnaz Faez and Michael Karas

Exploring the Principles of Reflective Practice in ELT: Research and Perspectives from Turkey
Edited by Bahar Gün and Evrim Üstünlüoğlu

Language Teacher Identity and Reflective Practice
Zia Tajeddin

Reflective Practice in TESOL Service-Learning
Cynthia Macknish

Surviving the Induction Years of Language Teaching: The Importance of Reflective Practice
Thomas S. C. Farrell

Teachers Reflecting on Boredom in the Language Classroom
Mirosław Pawlak, Mariusz Kruk and Joanna Zawodniak

The Reflective Cycle of the Teaching Practicum
Fiona Farr and Angela Farrell

Using Video to Support Teacher Reflection and Development in ELT

Laura Baecher, Steve Mann and Cecilia Nobre

SHEFFIELD UK   BRISTOL CT

Published by Equinox Publishing Ltd.
UK: Office 415, The Workstation, 15 Paternoster Row, Sheffield, South Yorkshire S1 2BX
USA: ISD, 70 Enterprise Drive, Bristol, CT 06010

www.equinoxpub.com

First published 2023

British Library Cataloguing-in-Publication Data
A catalogue record for this book is available from the British Library.

ISBN-13   978 1 78179 754 9   (hardback)
          978 1 78179 755 6   (paperback)
          978 1 78179 756 3   (ePDF)
          978 1 80050 318 2   (ePub)

Library of Congress Cataloging-in-Publication Data

Names: Baecher, Laura Hope, author. | Mann, Steve, 1960- author. | Nobre,
    Cecilia, author.
Title: Using video to support teacher reflection and development in ELT /
    Laura Baecher, Steve Mann and Cecilia Nobre.
Description: Sheffield, South Yorkshire ; Bristol, CT : Equinox Publishing
    Ltd, 2023. | Series: Reflective practice in language education |
    Includes bibliographical references and index. | Summary: "This book
    draws on a growing community of educators using video in a wide range of
    approaches and features some of their experiences and views through data
    and vignettes. In doing so, this text acts as a conduit for innovative
    and effective video and visual media use in language teacher
    education"-- Provided by publisher.
Identifiers: LCCN 2022042112 (print) | LCCN 2022042113 (ebook) | ISBN
    9781781797549 (hardback) | ISBN 9781781797556 (paperback) | ISBN
    9781781797563 (pdf) | ISBN 9781800503182 (epub)
Subjects: LCSH: English language--Study and teaching--Audio-visual aids.
Classification: LCC PE1067 .B34 2023 (print) | LCC PE1067 (ebook) | DDC
    428.0078--dc23/eng/20230106
LC record available at https://lccn.loc.gov/2022042112
LC ebook record available at https://lccn.loc.gov/2022042113

Typeset by Sparks Publishing Services Ltd – www.sparkspublishing.com

To my colleagues in the field of TESOL, near and far, present, and past. You have helped me 'see' and 'notice' and reflect. I thank you for the gift of collegiality.
Laura Baecher

To all my TESOL colleagues and students at University of Warwick especially the Hornby Scholars. You have all enriched my professional life.
Steve Mann

To all my Brazilian colleagues who have always supported me – in person and online. Your drive and enthusiasm motivates me.
Cecilia Nobre

Contents

Acknowledgements   viii

Series Editor's Preface   ix
Thomas S. C. Farrell

Introduction   1

Chapter 1: Video and Teacher Development   6

Chapter 2: The Context of Video Use   22

Chapter 3: Video as a Process and a Material in Learning about Teaching   38

Chapter 4: Learning to Look Descriptively at Teaching through Video   59

Chapter 5: Reflecting through Video: Self-Observation   79

Chapter 6: Video Observation with Peers   94

Chapter 7: Role of Video in Supervision   110

Chapter 8: Video in Research   129

References   145

Index   161

Acknowledgements

I would like to acknowledge the support and mentorship of Tom Farrell, whose confidence in me has energized my career and given life to this project.

Laura Baecher

I would like to thank the following for their help and ideas: Katie Webb, Maricarmen Gamero Mujica, Walaa Mouma, Claudia Bustos-Moraga, Mathew Turner, Jo Gakonga, Miriam Schwiening, Steve Walsh, Russell Stannard, Ross Crichton, Paul Miller, Adam Edmett, and especially Tom Farrell for his continuing guidance and friendship. Thanks to all the generous authors of vignettes in this book. To Addy Ahmad, Nusrat Gulzar, and Hanife Taşdemir, thank you for your time in proofreading the book.

Steve Mann

I would like to thank Tom Farrell, Laura Baecher, and Steve Mann for their guidance and support throughout the process of writing this book. As a novice writer, it was a steep learning curve.

Cecilia Nobre

Series Editor's Preface

Increasingly, language teachers, whether in training, or in-service, are expected to use and adapt digital resources in their teaching and so it makes sense for the language teacher education process to help familiarize them with important possibilities, constraints, and affordances. Language teacher educators also need to keep up-to-date and familiar with platforms, tools, apps, and online repositories and resources in order to support language teachers in materials development, adaptation, and use. *Using Video to Support Teacher Reflection and Development in ELT* by Laura Baecher, Steve Mann, and Cecilia Nobre is a timely book on a specific focus of reflection on the use of video as a tool in teacher learning, and teacher development. This is the first book of its kind that organizes a vast array of approaches into a user-friendly text so that educators can make greater use of this useful reflective tool.

The book outlines how teachers and teacher educators can introduce, design, implement, and assess video-based professional development through the concept of reflective practice. As such it is a natural fit into this series, *Reflective Practice in Language Education*. Indeed, their use of the word VIDEO as an acronym is an excellent example of the benefits of reflecting through video analysis; the acronym *VIDEO* stands for *V*isual, *I*nnovation, *D*evelopment, *E*ngagement, and *O*rganization. Throughout the book they outline a variety of ways in which digital video can support and encourage reflection, increase awareness, foster collaboration, share practice, provide a tool for analysis, help with materials production, and establish online communities of practice whether for teacher training or development. In addition, the authors make extensive use of a range of video practices currently in use by language teacher educators developed by one of the authors called *Video in Language Teacher Education* (ViLTE). Many of the current 31 ViLTE video case studies are also outlined and discussed in this book (see the ViLTE Project website (https://vilte.warwick.ac.uk/) for useful information, vignettes, transcripts of interviews, links, and research team profiles).

The book is organized into eight different chapters and includes the following useful features throughout each chapter: Templates to accompany video analysis tasks; Outlines of processes in a stepwise fashion; Vignettes from teacher educators who have used video; Application questions; Teacher Voices; Open-Access Video clips that can be utilized to implement the reflective tasks; and Reflective tasks throughout as well. Chapter 1, *Video and Teacher Development*, outlines and discusses the value of video in language teaching, teacher development, and language teacher education. Chapter 2, *The Context of Video Use*, discusses different contexts for video such as pre-service teacher education, the practicum, and in-service programs. Chapter 3, *Video As a Process and a Material in Learning About Teaching*, outlines videoconferencing in teacher development, production of videos in teacher education, as well as screencasting in teaching and teacher education. Chapter 4, *Learning to Look Descriptively at Teaching through Video*, discusses observation with videos using a scaffolded approach throughout. Chapter 5, *Reflecting through Video: Self-Observation*, outlines and discusses self-observation through video, while Chapter 6, *Video Observation with Peers*, outlines how peers can reflect through video. Chapter 7, *The Role of Video in Supervision*, outlines various combinations of how supervisors can use video in different settings. Chapter 8, *Video in Research*, outlines how video data can be collected for research purposes and how it can be used as a tool for disseminating research results. Throughout each chapter readers can find extensive examples of video as a reflective tool with direct links (i.e. various video-making tools and platforms, videoconferencing, video production, and screencasting, sites with videos of ELT, and many video projects, to name but a few) to how teachers, teacher educators, and students have successfully incorporated much of what the authors outline so that they will be able to make much progress in their own development as English language teachers regardless of the context in which they teach. In fact, this book provides such extensive information about the use of video as a reflection tool and it is essential reading for any educational setting that encourages the use of video analysis for whatever purpose. Probably for the first time, the contents of the chapters outlined above provide the most comprehensive introduction, description, and analysis of the use of video in any educational setting. It is truly a masterpiece for pre-service and in-service language teachers, language teacher educators, certificate students, as well as MA and PhD students, and teachers and teacher educators beyond language education. As series editor of the Equinox series, *Reflective Practice in Language Education*, I am honoured and excited they choose the series to publish their work.

Thomas S. C. Farrell

Series Editor, *Reflective Practice in Language Education*

Introduction

Over the last few decades, there has been an increase in both the use and understanding of the role digital video plays in supporting teacher development and in guiding reflective practice within teacher education. As educators, teachers, and authors, we are committed to working with video to help both teachers and learners. We hope to share some of our enthusiasm and concrete ideas for implementation in what follows.

Before we get to all that, let's start with some introductions:

Steve: When I first started teaching, around 40 years ago, there wasn't any video. There were a few TV programmes for education, and you could wheel in a TV to show a specific programme at a specific time. Later, there were video machines, and you could record TV programmes for subsequent use. However, the equipment was incredibly cumbersome and unreliable. Even in the 1990s access to good-quality English language video in most classrooms was extremely rare. Video, of course, was used as input (and only really in classrooms). Learners did not have the facilities to make their own video. Video production would have required large expensive cameras and a specialist sound equipment. Then, you'd need video-editing equipment, which was even rarer.

Years later, the scenario and choices look very different. Most learners have a video viewing, capture, and editing tool in their pockets. They learn through video, accessing YouTube, Tik Tok, and host of video choices. If they want to know about the life of a dolphin, know more about conjunctions, how to grow tomatoes, put a new battery in a MacBook, they can watch a video about it. Learners can capture, share, upload, re-edit, adapt, and tweak videos, annotate with text, and add pictures without much effort. Short videos become memes. They are part of the rich tapestry of our digital lives. Various free computer and mobile applications have made both synchronous and asynchronous F2F video communication across continents possible.

Although there remain challenges with bandwidth and internet connectivity, I believe this rapidly changing situation gives us some exciting choices and those older ones among us need to make sure we are not left behind, that we know how teaching and learning can be made more motivating, effective, and creative using video. I hope you enjoy this book and find new ways to use video in language teaching and education.

Laura: For me, using video as a teaching material meant getting a hold of the TV cart and pushing it through the school building, hoping you could get there in time. Once there, fast-forwarding to show clips of movies, turning off the sound so students could create their own dialogues, or turning the TV facing away from my class so they could only use the audio – thank you Susan Stempleski (1992)! – and practise listening skills. Students were always happy to see that big TV cart getting wheeled into the room as it equated with activities that relied less on the chalkboard and textbook. Somehow that medium of video automatically captivates students' eyes and ears.

But my strongest association with video in my career in ELT is its use for self-reflection and a window into classroom practice for teacher learning. When I started my MA in TESOL in the mid-1990s, our professor John Fanselow (1988) required us to use video… A lot! We might watch a 2-minute clip several times over in seminar class, record ourselves and write on what we saw, or be challenged to come up with a set of choices we could have made other than what we observed. Little did I know it then, but those early experiences with VHS tapes and bulky video cameras on tripods desensitized me to the presence of the camera and established a foundational belief that to understand my teaching, I needed to see it with my own eyes.

While the accessibility, portability, and ease of sharing video have made digitizing experiences part of our daily activities today, I believe that the approaches we take – not the technologies – make the strongest impact on our own and our English learners. I am hopeful that much of what you will find in this book will support you to continue to innovate and develop your practice, and that it is of use beyond the current platforms or tools.

Cecilia: My first official interest in video was during my Master's studies at the University of Warwick, where I decided to investigate how teachers used videos (self-observation, vlogs, and video club models) in their CPD. That's how I met Steve, he was my supervisor and I found out that our research interests were very similar. He was the first one to support me in researching how videos are used in teacher education programmes, which was something I have always been keen to understand. Videos are powerful tools and are here to stay and the opportunities for learning are almost unlimited: we can watch webinars live or recorded, we can watch a teacher sharing classroom ideas on Instagram, we can observe ourselves teaching, another teacher can observe us, we can watch an example of good teaching on YouTube…

I know teacher educators will find this book useful and extend their own practice (there are plenty of reflective tasks here!).

AIMS AND SCOPE

Currently, there are many research articles across a wide array of teacher education journals that present promising practices in video as a tool in teacher learning, but no practitioner-friendly text that organizes a variety of approaches for application in the field. We believe that this book will help educators to greatly expand their repertoire and confidence in introducing, designing, implementing, and assessing video-based professional development. This book focuses on the variety of ways in which video can support and encourage reflection, increase awareness, foster collaboration, share practice, provide a tool for analysis, help with materials production, and establish online communities of practice. When we use the term video, we are essentially talking about digital video, and the book presents and evaluates a range of practices where digital video is used. We are particularly interested in focusing on how video, screen-capture, and audio-visual tools and frameworks are used in innovative ways in teacher training and development.

We discuss examples of how video use can create a positive impact on trainees' and in-service teachers' engagement, motivation, and autonomy. Video allows more possibilities for context-sensitive noticing, editing, sharing, repackaging, and tagging, especially in combination with screen-capture software, and we detail many of these possibilities. There is an increasing array of tools that can be harnessed to support teacher learning and reflection. These can help to make aspects of classrooms, methodology, and learning more concrete and visible.

This book reviews and details video use in the field of language teacher education, while also referencing its use in other fields of education (e.g., maths teaching, health care). Across the chapters, the book draws on a growing community of teacher educators using video in a wide range of approaches and features some of their experiences and views through data and vignettes. In doing so, the book acts as a conduit for innovative and effective video and visual media use in language teacher education. This will enable reflection and further methodological development on areas of focus such as webinars, stimulated recall, video in peer observation, flipped training content, screen-capture feedback, video editing and analysis, captioning tools, and video for mentoring.

This book is primarily for teacher educators, teacher trainers, teacher leaders, and those with responsibility for ensuring high-quality pre-service teacher education and ongoing continuous professional development (CPD) options. We also aim to provide all educators with a full array of innovative possibilities from which they can draw when designing teacher learning and professional development initiatives using video records of teaching, as well as other tools and strategies for video use.

This book supports these activities in creative ways that can energize professional learning sessions. With this in mind, we include the following features:

1. Templates to accompany video analysis tasks
2. Outlines of processes in a stepwise fashion
3. Vignettes from teacher educators who have used video
4. Application questions
5. Teacher voices
6. Open-access video clips that can be utilized to implement the reflective tasks
7. Reflective tasks

This book draws on and extends the findings of the ViLTE project funded by the British Council. The ViLTE team (Andrew Davidson, Monika Davis, Tilly Harrison, Jo Gakonga, Maricarmen Gamero, Steve Mann, Penny Mosavian, Lynnette Richards) mapped the use of video in language teacher education and showcased examples of good practice through a publicly available website (https://vilte.warwick.ac.uk/). This book explains this project in more detail in Chapter 1.

Covid and Innovation

While we were writing this book, we were all hit by the Covid-19 pandemic. Despite all the well-documented and truly awful effects of this virus, it could be that for education there may be at least a few silver linings. As Baker wrote for the *Financial Times* (2020):

> This pandemic could profoundly change education for the better. Throughout history, the sector has been conservative and resistant to change. For centuries it had the slate, then came a century of blackboard and chalk. Now students are just a finger-click away from the vast knowledge of Google – so much greater than that of any individual teacher. Coronavirus has given schools Zoom, Microsoft Teams, and Google Classroom. The technology turns a laptop screen into a

classroom, where students and teachers see each other and can question each other in truly collaborative online learning.

While we would accept that this is somewhat a rosy view and that there are significant equity, expertise, and access issues for many teachers and learners, there seems little doubt that in the future, virtual classes could allow both students and teachers to learn and engage in development without always having to attend schools and training rooms. A movement towards blended/hybrid learning, flipped content, diversity, greater choice, and innovation will be accelerated. Video will have an important role to play in this movement.

We hope that you find this book valuable and that you have colleagues with whom you can discuss your ideas and reflections. We believe that reflection is always enriched through interaction, collaboration, and sharing. We have enjoyed working together, sharing ideas, drafts, and new tools and resources.

Chapter 1

Video and Teacher Development

INTRODUCTION

This opening chapter establishes the fundamental reasons *why* video is increasingly being used for language teacher development, thus providing a solid, research-informed rationale for the chapters which follow. We begin by presenting the value of video as a multimodal medium in any learning experience, then look at its role in language teaching. We then move on to overview the range of ways in which video can support teacher learning and reflective practice. We present key contributions from the growing literature, including important frameworks for conceptualizing and researching the contribution of video to teacher development. In presenting the rationale and research base for using video, this chapter highlights key arguments for the value of video for teacher learning.

THE VALUE OF VIDEO AS A MULTIMODAL LEARNING MATERIAL

We begin our consideration of the value of video in terms of *multimodality*, in order to differentiate it from the use of written text. Multimodality explicitly acknowledges multiple literacies within one medium, for example understanding that what is happening in a classroom involves understanding spoken and written language as well as any images displayed. Multimodality also encompasses movement, gestures, and non-verbal communication. Therefore, multimodality in learning contexts captures the full range of communication practices in terms of visual, textual, aural, linguistic, and spatial elements.

A multimodal form of delivery may lead to greater retention of information (Gellevij et al., 2002) because the use of two channels such as visual and auditory, instead of one, leads to greater retention of information. Video is automatically multimodal as it has several channels, combining visual images, audio, and perhaps some written text to reinforce key messages. When learning about teaching practice, video gives language teacher educators essential support in detailing, describing, noticing, and talking about classrooms beyond anything books, handouts, PDFs, and PowerPoint slides can offer. When teacher educators are interacting with teacher-learners, multimodality can also provide more channels through which communication can occur. As Kiddle and Prince (2019) put it, teacher and teacher trainer flexibility is inherently tied to multimodality:

> The primary area of flexibility lies in multi-modality; in the choice afforded by interacting through voice, video, text, and image, and the consequent opportunities for personalisation and contextualised appropriacy [to] allow participants to respond to content through webcam, microphone or text…This can be significant in terms of allowing culturally/contextually-appropriate interaction with course colleagues and tutors. (p. 113)

One of the prime ways that video is used in increasingly multimodal approaches relates to the reality that when we refer to 'video' we are using it as a shorthand primarily for digital video. This is not to say that VHS, BETA, CD-ROMs, and various other film and video formats have not been useful or might continue to be useful. However, the value of digital video is that it is more flexible and usable, in that it can be viewed on different devices, transferred, edited, and repurposed. This contributes to video being a multimodal material itself, and to its multimodal applications in teacher learning, expressed below using VIDEO as an acronym (**V**ision, **I**nnovation, **D**evelopment, **E**ngagement, **O**rganization).

As suggested in Figure 1.1, because video is seen as authentic and as giving greater access to the complexity of the classroom (including both verbal and paralinguistic features), teachers respond positively to its use, which impacts on their motivation, engagement, and autonomy (Gaudin & Chaliès, 2015). At the same time, evidence shows that efforts to integrate digital possibilities (e.g., video, e-portfolios) should be systematic and thoughtfully implemented (Kaya & Dikilitaş, 2019; Mann & Walsh, 2017). Teachers need to be familiar and comfortable with both the process and expectations of them when it comes to video use.

Reflective Break

1. In your experience learning to teach, how has video been used? Which of the VIDEO aspects do you believe you have experienced as a teacher-learner?
2. If you have worked as a teacher trainer or teacher educator, which of the VIDEO aspects above have you experienced?
3. In what ways has the multimodality of video as a material served your teacher learning needs?

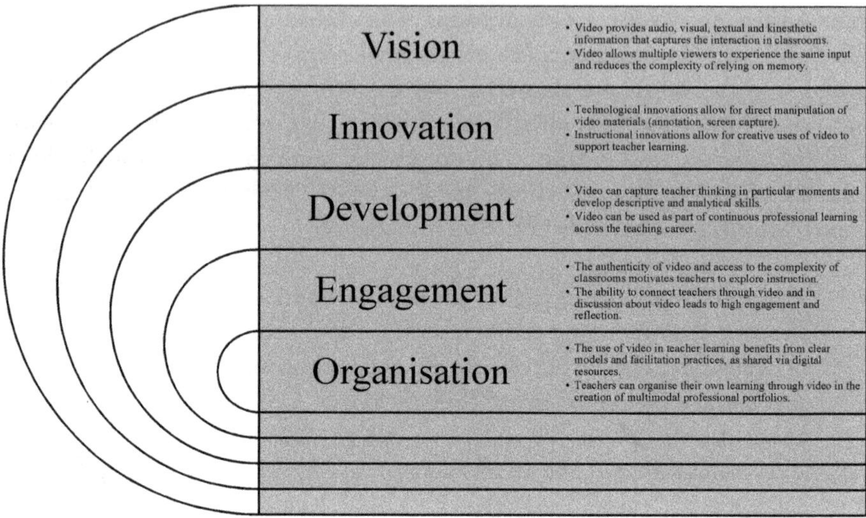

Figure 1.1. VIDEO in teacher learning.

VIDEO IN LANGUAGE TEACHING

This book is concerned with video in language teacher education and not directly with the role of video in language teaching; however, it is important that we note the use of video in language teaching for two important reasons: the need for teacher educators to model the use of video as a resource, and the parallel approaches of video in language lessons and in teacher education sessions.

First, language teachers are increasingly expected to use and adapt digital resources in their teaching and so it makes sense for the language teacher education process to help familiarize them with important possibilities, constraints, and affordances (see Murray & Christison, 2018). In short, it is important for teacher educators to practice what they preach. It does not make sense for a language teacher educator to lecture on the importance of technology and digital resources in a traditional chalk and talk manner. Teacher educators need to keep up-to-date and familiar with platforms, tools, apps, and online repositories and resources in order to support language teachers in materials development, adaptation, and use (Ally et al., 2014).

Second, language teachers readily recognize the multimodal benefits of using video as a language teaching material in their lessons, and this makes the transition to its use as a teacher learning material natural and more readily accepted. In a language lesson, video clips are presented, watched and re-watched, and analysed linguistically and paralinguistically. Students learn to notice and to become more language-aware through tasks that language teachers set to accompany the video material, and teacher educators use video in similar ways. While the content of the video in a language lesson might be a clip from a movie or an educational video, the content of video in language teacher education is likely to be a clip from an actual classroom scene or one the instructor has created for teacher-learners.

In the language teaching context, video has been used for many years in various formats but started to be used more and more with VHS and then CD-ROM options in the 1980s. It has been well-documented since the 1990s that there has been a noticeable increase in the use of video in language teaching (Goldstein & Driver, 2014). It is impossible to summarize these developments adequately here, but it is worth noting the sense of the scale of this growth. Language teaching coursebooks have increasingly integrated video since the early 1990s. Among the early adopters was *The Grapevine* series (1989–1992), where videos were a key part of language input. The BBC series 'English through Video' was also one of the first publications that was centred primarily on video content. Since then, other broadcasters (e.g., National Geographic) have invested heavily in packaging and re-editing content for language learning. Cooper et al.'s *Video* (1991) is a good start in considering how an active and task-based methodology around video was established.

Lonergan (1984) was one of the first to articulate the benefits of video for language learning, stating that video allows access to 'complete communicative situations' where students can be supported by their teachers in watching and listening to fluent speakers. Through video, the language learner can 'readily see the ages of the participants; their sex; perhaps their relationships to one to another; their dress, social status and what they are doing; and perhaps their mood or feelings' (p. 18). Video also offers paralinguistic information, such as facial expressions or hand gestures which provide more contextual clues beyond the audio alone. There have been a series of publications that built on the early work of Cooper and Lonergan. They have suggested how language teachers can use video in effective and practical ways, further making the argument that video provides authentic language, verbal and contextual language features, paralinguistic and non-verbal dimensions, and increased engagement and motivation.

In addition to a realization that video has intrinsic benefits, there has been a recognition that structured viewing guides can assist the language teacher in tapping into these benefits. Guides, such as Stempleski and Tomalin's *Film* (2001) and Sherman's (2003) contribution on the value of 'authentic video' in the language classroom, contain practical suggestions for activities built upon the principle of active, structured, and guided viewing tasks. Later in the book, we will return to this important concept in considering how particular video-based tasks require teachers to be both active and data-led. For now, and in terms of language learning, there was an important realization that although video brings the potential for a concrete and specific point of reference and an engaging context, it also comes with the risk of learners being passive. The importance of facilitation and not simply presenting and standing by has consistently been important in the use of video as a material.

In recent years a number of influential ELT trainers (e.g., Peachey & Hockly) have championed the use of video and digital tools. Peachey (2015) provides a unique multimedia manual for language teachers that gives advice about activities, courses, and developing engaging materials. It is particularly helpful in offering advice about mobile apps on handheld devices and tips for building video in blended and task-based ways in language teaching contexts. Hockly (2018) has advocated for caution and consideration when language teachers bring images and video technologies into the language learning classroom and called for explicit attention to digital literacy as a topic for language teaching.

Other recent publications have consolidated the view that video use is an important and growing tool for language teaching and learning. Goldstein and Driver's *Language Learning with Digital Video* (2014), Keddie's *Bringing Online Video into the Classroom* (2014), and Donaghy's *Film in Action* (2015) have all successfully established this video agenda. Donaghy and Xerri's edited collection *The Image in English Language Teaching* (2017) has useful contributions to the history and value of video in language learning. In this edited collection, Whitcher (2017) talks about her work with Donaghy establishing what they call a 'visual manifesto' which calls for more intentionality and reflection when working with video and imagery. It also addresses the challenge of helping video-viewers to be active, reflective, selective, and autonomous. In the same collection, Goldstein (2017) provides a history of video in ELT and considers what role it will play in the future, and Clare (2017) examines why video is such an engaging language learning tool. These chapters provide invaluable background information about the link between video and language acquisition.

All of these authors have established the educational value of digital video in language teaching and learning and shifted the balance from video as input to embracing the idea that language learners can make their own video. In relation to language learning, Jarvis (2015) gives examples of the range of activities in which mobile technologies can play an important role in consolidating language and enhancing motivation. For example, students can use mobile devices to take photos or videos at home. These artefacts then become the basis for sharing and discussion between learners.

Making video is inevitably more active than consuming video and this is crucial from the SLA dimension. Not only does the process around making video offer the potential for negotiated interaction, but the actual video then becomes a form of output. Video can also be used as the basis through which language learners communicate, as through videoconferencing. Therefore, we should distinguish between *viewing video*, *making video*, and *communicating through video* in understanding the value and potential of video. The EU-funded project 'Video for All' established the importance of this distinction in two video resource handbooks for language teachers and teacher educators: MacKinnon and Mann (2016) and Hottman (2016).

As well as activities that make use of existing video content available on sites such as YouTube and Vimeo, language students are now much more likely to watch music videos, cartoons, and short-form video outside classrooms (Copland et al., 2012) and sites such as Stannard's TTV (http://www.teachertrainingvideos.com/) show teachers how to use various apps and online resources. A good example of a video-based tool would be the *Lyrics Training* website (https://lyricstraining. com/), where language learners can choose their level to improve both listening and writing skills based around song lyrics. There are many resources online for language teachers looking for video content that has embedded tasks alongside it, such as 100+ Must-See Video Sites for Educators (https://www.teachthought. com/pedagogy/100-must-see-video-sites-for-educators/), 10 free quality video resources for teachers (https://www.bookwidgets.com/blog/2018/05/10-free-quality-video-resources-for-teachers), and 7 Great Resources for Any Kind of Language Teaching Video | General Educator Blog (https://www.fluentu.com/blog/educator/language-teaching-videos/).

Reflective Break
Pre-watching reflection
1. Reflect on how many images you see and videos you watch in an average week.

Watch the video
2. A Visual Manifesto for Language Teaching, https://vimeo.com/113420504.

Post-watching reflection
3. Why is it important to get learners to look critically at images and videos?
4. How can this be achieved in language teaching?
5. How can students be positioned less as consumers of video and more as producers of video content? What impact would that have on their language learning?

Continuing forward with the idea of making one's own video in addition to consuming published video materials, language teachers, like their students, can also be producers of video content. This is exemplified in the following vignette, which raises important themes about both fostering assessment and reflection. In this case, a language teacher creates her own video of her students' oral production in order to use that video for the students to better understand their performance. Most reports of video for language learning purposes suggest that students quickly get used to this way of working and that (with permission) a video bank can help prepare students with good examples of presentations and in the formulation of tips and advice (Mann et al., 2019).

Vignette

Emma Almingefeldt

Faculty of Librarianship, Information, Education and IT, University of Borås, Sweden

Equal assessment and a tool for improvement of speech

Student: Can you please explain to me why I didn't pass the oral examination?

Teacher: I couldn't understand what you said.

Student: What didn't you understand?

Teacher: The thing is since I didn't understand what you said I am sorry to say that I can't tell you where you went wrong (Almingefeldt, 2019a, 2019b)

This conversation with one of my second language students made me think that if I had videoed the oral examination, I could have reviewed the examination together with my student and I would have been able to point out exactly what is needed to improve when it comes to pronunciation, vocabulary, and grammar.

Along with my co-workers, we began to video students attending second language classes at the University of Borås (designed for international students and for academic immigrant students). We wanted to be able to see if the video would be a good tool to implement for language teachers when it comes to making sure that exams are conducted fairly and in accordance with guidelines surrounding students' rights to be assessed equally.

Consequently, we videoed the students during their oral exams. Depending on the exam, sometimes it was done individually and sometimes in small groups. Before we could start filming, we had to make sure it was done with consent. Consent was solved by getting the students to sign a document, and before doing so they had been very well informed of their rights and the reason for the recording. Five out of over 200 students turned down the offer of being filmed during their oral examinations. A few said no at the beginning of the exam but when it was their turn, they changed their minds. Later consent has been solved by writing in the course plan that the examination might be video and so no documents need to be signed and archived.

For videoing, we needed a tool that had a very good microphone that wouldn't disturb and be in the way of the students, and especially since we were mostly interested in being able to go back and listen again, we needed a microphone with good sound quality. We also needed a tool that would let us save our recordings for many years since there is no limit of time when a university student in Sweden can appeal a grade. Swivl (www.swivl.com) was found to be a tool that met all our requirements.

Over 200 second language learners have been asked about their experiences being filmed. The result shows that 93% of the students reported positive or neutral feelings about the recordings. Very specific and detailed feedback can be given about a word, sentence, or utterance. Students themselves are able to listen to what they actually said and reflect upon what they did well and what they have to focus on to do better:

> *When I watched my film and read the comments, I totally understood why it didn't pass.*

The results also indicate that students find oral examinations to have a higher status if they are videoed and are fairer when it comes to assessment and grading:

> *I think it is needed for perfect scoring.*

Six teachers have been interviewed and the findings reveal that the teacher can focus on the examination/presentation/discussion, instead of taking notes, and it was easier for the examiner to get a second opinion from another teacher. One teacher said:

> *I feel less stressed when I know I can go back and listen once more. It seems like less students question my assessment compared to when I didn't film my students.*

For us, the findings show that video is a useful tool that benefits both students and teachers when it comes to fairer assessment and speech training in language education.

This vignette offers an important link between video in language teaching and teacher development. While the language teacher in this case created a video of a language learner for the audience of that same language learner – in this example to bring awareness of their spoken output—it also was a form of feedback for the language teacher. By having a chance to capture, rewind, and review her student's performance, she could refine her teaching approaches and improve her instruction. Although teacher education needs to make teachers aware of the potential of video in language learning, we are more concerned in this book with the potential of video for supporting teacher learning, reflection, and development. In this next section, we provide a general overview of how video can be used to inform language teacher development, and there is an abundance of work in this area, as you will see in the chapters that follow.

VIDEO IN LANGUAGE TEACHER DEVELOPMENT

Video, with its inherently multimodal nature, is a tool that offers a greater ability to capture the detail of classroom interaction than a written description. Sert (2019) argues that published extracts may not be as effective as video materials that provide rich audio-visual input. Although activities based around transcripts and written descriptions are undoubtedly useful, such activities and tasks in teacher education programmes are not as helpful as video in increasing awareness of interaction. There is further evidence that video is more helpful than audio recordings. For example, Calandra et al. (2018) compared the quality of reflection when teachers were prompted by video and when they were prompted by audio. All reflection papers were evaluated using a rubric developed by Ward and McCotter (2004). They found that participants wrote significantly higher quality papers across several indicators when prompted by video (rather than when prompted by audio).

> **Vignette: Overcoming Initial Challenges in Training Courses Amid COVID**
> *Taylor Veigga*
> *Trinity DipTESOL and CertTESOL Teacher Trainer, Brazil*
>
> The pandemic hit Brazil very hard and there were many doubts about the efficacy of teacher education courses that were fully online. I believe nowadays this is no longer an issue, and people do not question the validity of such programmes any more. The beginning was certainly challenging. Observing and assessing video lessons was something many teacher educators were not comfortable doing. As I had been teaching online before COVID, I could see some advantages there, and I remember trying to convince others that a camera in a classroom

was less intimidating than an observer for both teachers and students alike. In these video observations, we could rewind and rewatch something whenever it was not clear, but there were downsides too. Camera placement had to be very strategic so as to cover most of the room, and it was difficult to hear teachers at times, especially when they were wearing masks.

The live online lessons had their own challenges too. Some students would not keep their cameras on all the time or not have them on at all. If teaching is hard, imagine teaching black squares on Zoom while having your lesson assessed at the same time. We as teacher educators would always reassure teachers and make it clear to them this was beyond their control, telling them that, sometimes, nothing could be done. Nowadays I see many similarities with that and face-to-face teaching and training. There is always something that cannot be controlled, and we have to make the most with what we have, and video has certainly been an essential tool for teacher educators in the online environment.

Mann et al. (2019) catalogued an extensive range of video practices currently in use by language teacher educators. Their project *Video in Language Teacher Education* (ViLTE) was funded by the British Council ELT Research Partnership Awards Scheme and was undertaken during 2017 and 2018. Its main aims were: (1) to map the current use of video and visual media tools in language teacher education and (2) to build a community of practice among practitioners involved in teacher education in order to share good practice. A published report (available at Video in language teacher education https://www.teachingenglish.org.uk/sites/teacheng/files/J201%20ELT%20Video%20in%20language%20teacher%20education%20FINAL_Web.pdf) primarily concerned the first of these aims. The second aim was realized through the following web resources: the ViLTE Project website https://vilte.warwick.ac.uk/ (useful information, vignettes, transcripts of interviews, links, research team profiles) and ViLTE Video case studies (videos featuring various video-based practices, https://vilte.warwick.ac.uk/collections/show/1). The ViLTE project also encouraged postgraduate researchers to join the project, and this resulted in substantial and original work (see Gamero, 2017; Gulzar, 2018; Nobre, 2018a; Phan, 2017).

The ViLTE Video case studies currently have 31 video contributions, with more planned for the future. The study uncovered considerable diversity in video use in language teacher education. The role that video plays in training is primarily as input (to model, explain, prompt discussion), and there is growing evidence that digital media makes it possible for this video content to be used in active and reflective ways. In summary, the report details a range of video practices as highlighted in Table 1.1.

Table 1.1. A survey of ViLTE video cases

Viewing a variety of classrooms	ViLTE provides a wide-ranging list of resources (https://warwick.ac.uk/fac/soc/al/research/vilte/resources/websites_for_video.pdf) that teacher educators are currently using to view different classrooms.
Watching videos of one's own and others' classrooms	Balancing of watching own or peer videos and those featuring other teachers is crucial. Pianta et al. (2014) argue that watching video classroom interactions is of particular value.
Video for self-evaluation and peer evaluation	Video provides 'a fine-grained multimodal record of an event' (Jewitt, 2012, p. 2) and this can provide a catalyst for both self- and peer evaluation.
Video platforms	Increased use of platforms (e.g., VEO and IRIS Connect) make video viewing systematic, user-friendly, and reliable. ViLTE provides a list of platforms (https://warwick.ac.uk/fac/soc/al/research/vilte/resources/video_platform_options/) (e.g., OnVu, Panopto) that are currently being used by educators.
Video for stimulated recall research	Video-stimulated interviewing has become an important tool in educational research (Nguyen et al., 2013).
Distance mentoring	Video makes it possible to offer mentoring and coaching remotely (either in a blended way or by distance).
Video in online training	Online training increasingly relies on video, either in introductory videos or for real-time contact (through Zoom or Skype). A sense of physical presence and familiarity online is crucial, and video increases the sense of the tutor presence in the course (see Olesova & Borup, 2016).
VR and 360	There are some promising developments in the use of virtual reality (VR) and '360 videos' in teacher training and development (e.g., Driver, 2017).
Screencasting	There is increasing use of screencasting and screen-capture software in teacher education (e.g., Mahoney et al., 2019).
Making videos	Teacher educators are increasingly making their own videos in addition to curating OER video resources and purchasing professionally made third-party videos.
Remote video-teaching	There is an important and emerging area, particularly if access to high-quality teaching resources on the ground is limited (e.g., Plan Ceibal (https://www.ceibal.edu.uy/es) and HandsUP projects (https://www.teachingenglish.org.uk/article/hands-project)).
Video banks/resources	Individual and institutional attempts to put together a bank of classroom videos for teacher development (e.g., ViLTE at University of Southampton).
Video in e-portfolios	The last decade has seen a growth in research on how such tools as electronic portfolios (e-portfolios) can be employed to foster reflection in both PRESET and INSET teachers (e.g., Cherrington & Loveridge, 2014).
Webinars and videoconferencing	Webinars allow a focused and specific topic for professional development (PD) to be presented by more experienced colleagues or well-known figures in the field. An important feature of PD webinars is the sense of community and connection to other teachers.

Although the focus of this book is on language teacher education, it is important to recognize that the use of video technologies for the professional development of teachers has been explored in other areas (e.g., science and mathematics teaching). They have established that digital video is a highly promising tool for engaging teachers in reflections about their own teaching strategies. In the Best Foot Forward Project (https://warwick.ac.uk/fac/soc/al/research/vilte/resources/kane_et_al_2015.pdf), Kane et al. (2015) present three critical reasons for using video in teacher reflection: (1) teachers cannot notice everything happening in classrooms; (2) they cannot think deeply about cause and effect when making in-the-moment instructional decisions, and (3) they cannot remember everything that occurred. Video use helps teachers learn how to describe without judgement, use those descriptions to analyse learning and classroom events, and then move onto a greater focus on concrete aspects rather than an overly general and descriptive reflection response (Star & Strickland, 2008; Stockero, 2008; Sydnor, 2016).

In general terms, mathematics teacher education has established that pre-service teachers' reflections reach higher levels with the employment of video resources (Harford et al., 2010). Video analysis can also assist teachers in shifting from their personal recall and embodied experience in the lesson to focusing on issue of student behaviour, engagement, and learning (Santagata, 2014). Yeh and Santagata (2015) throw further light on working with pre-service mathematics teachers and getting them to form hypotheses based on video evidence (see also Forest & Mercier, 2011; Santagata & Yeh, 2014). They report that it is much more useful to show some visualization sequences of teachers' actions (taken from video recording) than to give them a lecture about teaching gestures and their effectiveness. In fact, it is hard to find a paper that does not support a position that teachers value video and that it enables engagement, collaboration, and reflection (although see Stokes et al., 2020).

It is undoubtedly the case that most studies on video use have been conducted in the USA and Canada or Europe, but there are a few accounts of the value of video for teachers in other contexts. Lok et al. (2018) is a good example in Cambodia, where they report on the effectiveness of using video to introduce student-centred teaching to teachers through training that involved collaboratively watching and discussing videos of teaching practices. Mann et al. (2020), in the Thai context, confirmed that video clips enabled focused talk and reflection on Thai language learning classrooms and that videos allow opportunities for meaningful and concrete discussion and opportunities to observe and articulate connections between theory and practice (see also Asanok & Chookhampaeng, 2016; McAleavy et al., 2018).

A growing number of teacher educators make use of video recordings of classroom events as one of their most reliable and valuable resources. If the recordings are of individual teachers, the video provides a personal, engaging, and powerful record of classroom events that teachers do not need to try and recall. Perhaps one of the most important values of video is that teachers can come back to the record after the class is over and do so with other viewers. In this way, teachers have the opportunity to re-enter the moment and reflect on classroom decisions, away from the demands of the classroom (Sherin, 2007). The video record assists in creating new opportunities to notice classroom events that might have escaped the teacher's attention in the moment. Researchers have found that discussion and reflection around video extracts is an especially useful way to scaffold trainer learning (e.g., Brunvand & Fishman, 2006) and such a process is engaging and fosters reflection (Mann et al., 2019).

Video can be used as input or reference material and can be used whether the teacher education programme is F2F, blended, or distance. Whatever the context, the use of video can help make learning to teach as active a process as possible. We can make an important distinction between video as input (consistent with a transmission approach) or as a tool for reflection and discussion (more consistent with a constructivist approach). This is not an either/or choice and good training is often a mixture of explanation, instruction, tasks, and opportunities for reflection (Edge, 2011). However, our view is that the challenge for most teacher educators is to reduce the abstracted talk about teaching and find ways to engage teachers in interaction, reflection, and co-construction directly with teaching.

RESEARCH AND FRAMEWORKS FOR THE USE OF VIDEO IN LANGUAGE TEACHER EDUCATION

There have been a number of meta-analyses of the literature, with Brophy (2004) providing the first comprehensive attempt to summarize the categories of video use in teacher education. He established that teacher training can include micro-teaching, modelling expert teaching, interaction analysis, video-based cases, hypermedia programs, and field recordings of teaching practice. These kinds of videos facilitate a process where teachers can notice the more subtle features of classrooms (such as non-verbal expressions of teacher–student or student–student interactions). His main argument was that this information is not so available in written text or in simple explanations or narratives and this is a theme we will explore further later in the book.

Gaudin and Chaliès' meta-review of the literature (2015) shows that video viewing is a unique and potentially powerful tool in teacher education. Their findings underline that 'the value of video use by teachers lies principally in the opportunity to raise teachers' quality of instruction and concomitantly to modernize education'

(p. 59). Gaudin and Chaliès (2015) point to two main reasons for the growth of video in teacher education. First, videos give teachers access to the classroom, which helps establish a link between the traditional theoretical education at the university and classroom practice (Clarke, 1994). Secondly, video viewing has been greatly eased by technical progress (e.g., digitalization, storage, edition, and annotation). Improved storage capacities and sophisticated software have all helped to embed video in the framework of teacher education. The Gaudin and Chaliès review collected and summarized 255 articles. They conceptualized the articles according to four aspects: teachers' activity as they view a classroom video, the objectives of video viewing, the types of videos viewed, and the effects of video viewing on teacher education and professional development. They also suggest three questions that may profitably guide future research: (1) How can teaching teachers to identify and interpret relevant classroom events on video clips improve their capacity to perform the same activities in the classroom?; (2) How can we best articulate the diverse objectives of video viewing and the diverse types of videos in teacher education and professional development programs?; and (3) How can we create a 'continuum' between teacher education programs and professional development with video?

Major and Watson (2018) also provide a thorough review showing how video has been increasingly used to support teacher professional development. They argue that advances in affordability and usability of technology mean that interest is bound to develop further. The authors use a scoping review approach (based on a review of 82 studies). They use these studies to produce a thematic overview of the effect of video on teacher cognition and classroom instruction. They argue that most research has been qualitative in nature and that there is a need for more quantitative research to identify how the use of video impacts on actual classroom practices. Hockly (2018) also provides a timely overview of the reasons why the use of video recordings of classroom practice appears to be an effective vehicle for supporting and developing reflection and analysis for teachers.

Baecher et al. (2018b) is a recent and systematic review of video analysis related to classroom practice, looking at over 100 articles published in a five-year period between 2012–2016. They track the increasing use of video as a tool in teacher professional learning and show how, in education design terms, video is now seen as a key part of professional development for teachers. Their review categorises the type and focus of video observation as well as the teachers' and facilitators' activities as they view classroom video. They find that while numerous studies have been published that consistently show the positive impact of video analysis on teacher learning, very few explicitly outline the steps the facilitators engaged in, making these studies impossible to replicate. They call for a greater degree of transparency in reporting on video use studies in teacher education so that practitioners and scholars can attempt to implement the specific practices that appear to lead to successful outcomes.

In addition to useful reviews, it is helpful to consider the role of useful frameworks in making the most out of video resources. Gelfuso (2016) builds on the work of Clara (2015) to put forward a framework that establishes the importance of 'warranted assertability' – where evidence from video provides the warrant. In other words, 'a successful reflection ends with such warranted assertability and a corresponding move from analysis to synthesis' (Gelfuso, 2016, p. 68). Reflection is more evidence-based and data-led if it is tied to a tangible moment or incident, and assertions, articulations, and arguments are therefore more warranted and grounded with video.

Such a data-led approach is consistent with frameworks for reflective practice, namely those by Farrell (2008, 2014, 2022), Mann and Walsh (2017) and Walsh (2020).

There has been some success in the use of frameworks to focus on aspects of teacher talk. For example, the Video Enhanced Observation (VEO) tool has been adapted to tag talk according to the SETT (Self-Evaluation of Teacher Talk) framework (Walsh, 2018). This combination of the tool (VEO) which captures, stores, and allows tagging/annotation of video and the framework (SETT), which informs the tag-set, has helped develop teachers' classroom communicative competence. Seedhouse's latest book *Video Enhanced Observation for Language Teaching* (2021) provides comprehensive studies, frameworks, and cases on how a VEO (www.veo. co.uk) can foster reflection and professional development in different teaching scenarios. Each chapter was written by experts in educational technology and applied linguistics who use the VEO app to tag, analyse, and evaluate talk and other teachable moments within teaching and training.

Video has been found to help teachers gain closer understandings of the complex relationship between language, interaction, and learning (see Bozbıyık, 2017). It is particularly helpful for interactional features (such as clarification requests, display questions, teacher echo). Another example of a useful framework is the LOCIT (Lesson Observation and Critical Incident Technique) video-stimulated model that has been used by Coyle (e.g., 2007) and others. LOCIT aims at helping teachers to undertake practitioner research and dialogic reflection through class-based exploration and the identification of 'learning moments'. Coyle and colleagues (2007) have a particular research focus on developing spatial awareness in pre-service teachers and the need to evidence how space (inside, outside and across physical boundaries) impacts on learner attainment, achievement, and sense of self-worth.

Hüttner (2019) identifies the main reasons why video has proved valuable in engaging teachers in noticing and learning in complex situations. Hüttner notes that video provides a lasting record of teaching practice, which can be viewed repeatedly and paused, so allowing for a selection of focus on the part of the student teachers and teacher educators, as well as a reduction of the demands of remembering a lesson observed or taught live. Video can be edited and collected so that video libraries of teaching specific aspects can be created and made accessible. Video allows for an observation of alternative practices; those in different contexts or following different curricula and/or frameworks, and so expands the range of pedagogical choices that teachers are confronted with and can alleviate pressure on local schools in terms of visiting student teachers and bypass any difficulties in accessing schools for lesson observation.

Marsh and Mitchell (2014) say that, overall, we can see that videos allow access to:

> complex 'thick' descriptions of classroom dynamics that are hard or impossible to access or describe in other ways. In other words, video sequences allow for viewers to follow the unfolding of complex social events over time, watching, for example, how teachers employ strategies for dealing with diverse classroom situations. (p. 404)

This can be especially helpful in talking about transitions, stages, and lesson flow (Tardy & Snyder, 2004). To summarize the value of video, its undoubted benefit is that it enables teachers to step back into their practice as observers and notice issues in their teaching which they could not recall from memory or which they had not attended to during their lesson, re-engaging with particular moments and incidents (Tripp & Rich, 2012). Research has highlighted the importance and role of video in language teacher training and development, and video is increasingly used to support both pre-service and in-service teacher professional development. The remaining chapters of this book will focus on various aspects of video in teacher learning contexts.

Reflective Break

1. Why is video powerful in language teacher education? Make a list of four or five features that video has that written text lacks that are important in a teacher education programme.
2. If you have trained teachers or taught online, how can video support your role in the online teaching environment?
3. What do the meta-analyses of the literature on video analysis in teacher learning suggest as areas for further research in this area?
4. Think about some videos that you curated to use in your classroom. Why did you choose to use them? How did your students engage with them?

Chapter 2

The Context of Video Use

INTRODUCTION

In Chapter 1, we explored *why* video has been such a powerful tool in the professional development of educators and key reasons for its widespread adoption. At the same time, we recognize that just as 'one size fits all' professional development packages do not take into account that educator learning always takes place in a particular context, video should be appropriately situated within its local setting. The importance of context is the focus of this chapter, and we consider the relationship between context (*where* the video use will be taking place) and the actors (*who* will be making video-based choices and *who* will be engaged in the learning process). Our goal in this chapter is to connect particular language training contexts to appropriate selection of video materials and methodology. We begin with a review of the social constructivist theories that undergird the approaches that are described, examine contexts from pre-service teacher education to short-term certificate programmes, to full Master's and in-service teacher development programmes, and conclude with how video cases offer rich opportunities to position video as situated learning materials.

CONTEXT AND CONSTRUCTIVISM IN LEARNING THROUGH VIDEO

Throughout this book, we are informed by constructivist learning theory. We recognize that teacher training and development is a social and situated process and see knowledge as negotiated and co-constructed in these specific teacher education contexts (Walsh, 2011). The nature of this co-construction varies from context to context and particularly depends on whether facilitators see their role as one of transmission or enabling dialogic reflection (Walsh & Mann, 2015), although most educators are trying to arrive at the appropriate balance of both roles. In either case, the idea of drawing on and promoting a community of practice around digital video recognizes that knowledge is grounded in the contexts and constraints of practice (Lave & Wenger, 1991). Video can both help to engage language teachers in a data-led process of reflection within a social context and help them to focus on the negotiated and co-constructed aspects of language classrooms and learning.

One of the most influential perspectives on learning and professional development which embraces the notion of collaboration and co-construction is the socio-cultural learning perspective. Socio-cultural theories emphasize the social nature of learning, which takes place as learners interact with another with greater expertise, and these social interactions lead to understanding (Roehler & Cantlon, 1997). The core tenet of this view is that learners collectively and actively construct their knowledge by making connections, building mental schemata and concepts through collaborative meaning-making in a specific context. In other words, the socio-cultural learning approach believes teachers must embody opportunities for dialogic mediation, scaffolded learning, and assistance performance to fully learn aspects of their teaching (Johnson, 2009).

While we value notions such as co-construction and collaboration, sometimes video will be used more directively to demonstrate, inform, and illustrate choices and options. For instance, Edge's (2011) CATRA model includes *copying, applying, theorizing, reflecting,* and *acting,* which closely parallels Grossman et al.'s (2009) cycle of teacher learning that includes the phases of *representation, decomposition,* and *approximation.* These suppose that teacher preparation does require 'showing' models of practice that teacher-learners can replicate. Although we should be critical of the idea of 'best practice', it is often helpful for novice teachers to see some examples of good teaching from local contexts. Especially in the early stages of training and development, teachers will benefit from such models and guidance. This practice of showing good teaching through video is common in initial teaching programmes such as the CELTA and the CertTESOL.

In both Grossman's and Edge's models of teacher learning, video has a critical role to play as a material in the introduction of the pedagogy and the simulation of it, but also in the enactment and reflection stages. Rather than waiting for practicum when teachers will finally 'apply theory', student teachers engage with theory in practice and arrive at theory from practice from the *beginning* of their programmes. Video can be used to show, demonstrate, foster discussion, provide data for reflection, enable peer discussion and reflection – in simple terms, as food in a varied diet.

Socio-cultural theory and the overlapping perspective of constructivism provide a paradigm within which educators engage in a detailed discussion of video use. In this regard, video helps to engage teacher-learners in noticing and learning in complex situations. It is thus particularly well-suited for supporting novice teachers' learning and raising their awareness. For example, a novice teacher might capture a full one-hour lesson on video, then edit out one or two 5-minute excerpts to bring to a mentor conversation, and then work together through their exchange to externalize existing and developing teaching insights (e.g., Calandra et al., 2009).

> **Reflective Break**
> 1. Socio-cultural theory suggests that learning is mediated through objects and through interactions with others. How can you envision video being used as an object in this approach?
> 2. How is learning through video especially tied to contextual factors? What might those factors consist of?

PRE-SERVICE TEACHER EDUCATION CONTEXTS

Right from the start of a teacher education programme, it is a good idea to introduce video, as there is growing evidence that video-based reflective practice (RP) can pave the way for subsequent collaborative and data-focused analysis in the professional learning of pre-service teachers. For example, a recent study by Yuan et al. (2020) explored how pre-service language teachers, from the early stages of their programme, engaged in video-based RP followed by a series of collaborative tasks (e.g., joint lesson planning and group consultation). Video-based RP in their study was also applied to a micro-teaching activity, which was video-recorded and followed by peer reflection. They investigated to what extent and how video-based RP contributed to these pre-service teachers' professional learning. Their findings were largely positive, and they claim that video-based RP helped student teachers learn to manage and regulate their own learning process and outcomes. Other studies show that pre-service teachers' self-reflections were more detailed in the video-based condition and self-reflections displayed a higher level of knowledge-based reasoning (Baecher & Kung, 2011; Estapa et al., 2016; Prilop et al., 2019).

As pre-service teachers move into their programme, there is a general agreement that they greatly benefit from viewing classrooms and language learners in action (Santagata & Guarino, 2011). Most pre-service teacher education programmers include some element of schools visit and observation, usually before the practicum. Traditionally, this was achieved through actual visits to schools and there is undoubtedly continuing value in this practice (Arthur et al., 2010). However, the availability of video recordings of classrooms enables additional and supplementary possibilities, not least because there is no limit to how many students can view them and that they can be viewed and reviewed. Especially in an era where school visits are limited due to public health concerns, 'video visits' serve an essential function in allowing pre-service teachers to witness classroom interactions. Mann et al. (2019) include an interview with Alan Pulverness (https://warwick.ac.uk/fac/soc/al/research/vilte/resources/interview_summaries/alan_pulverness_-_interview_summary.pdf), who works at the Norwich Institute for Language Education (NILE), on the variety of ways he has used video to focus on classrooms. He uses video because it is 'a convenient way for them not to have to do face-to-face observation but has become an interesting task in itself'. This has been partly 'a response to the practical demands of being able to set up a sufficient number of hours of live observation'. A great deal of observation can happen at NILE, but video provides the option of fulfilling the required hours for observation.

Over the years, there have been useful VHS and CD-ROM resources which have enabled teacher educators to integrate video examples of classroom practice, whether focusing on techniques or more general advice. The International House video series (Carr & Lynch, 2006) has been well used on a range of courses and several methodology books (for example, Scrivener, 2011 and Harmer, 2015 have increasingly made video a key part of their design). The ViLTE project interviewed Harmer (https://warwick.ac.uk/fac/soc/al/research/vilte/resources/interview_summaries/jeremy_harmer_-_interview_summary.pdf) and Scrivener (https://warwick.ac.uk/fac/soc/al/research/vilte/resources/interview_summaries/jim_scrivener_-_interview_summary.pdf) on aspects of including video content in training books and these interviews are good insights into some of the real-world challenges of filming appropriate video content. In this interview, Scrivener says:

> Macmillan originally wanted just the short clips, but I argued strongly for a longer lesson. You need to see how small bits come together/how a whole coherent lesson breaks down into small pieces. I would've liked to have more longer lessons from different teachers at different levels. I think you do need to see how small bits come together or how a big thing is broken down into small pieces whichever way you want to view it. Whether its small bits that add up or big bits that can be analysed down. I think it's best for you to see an example of what a whole relatively coherent lesson looks like, how a teacher handles not just the bravo moment but the small changes between things, how a teacher deals with something when somebody doesn't give the answer they expect. That sort of stuff. All the things that wouldn't be captured maybe in little techniques.

Hüttner (2019) recognizes that it can be very helpful to use video 'as a means of presenting standard teaching practice, implicitly often assumed to be an ideal' (p. 476), and this is the rationale underlying many commercially available teaching videos, such as the ones included in teacher-training books (e.g., Harmer, 2015; Thaler, 2012) produced by commercial language teacher-training companies. As Hüttner (2019) highlights:

> A common feature of such resources is quite extensive editing, frequently cutting out or shortening any non-teacher-led activities, like group work. This predisposes the viewers towards a focus on the teacher and their actions. The resource creators explicitly brand these videos as showing examples of 'best practice' teaching, often focused on either quite general approaches or methods (e.g., Task-Based Language Teaching) or specific skills (e.g., listening), or uses of new technologies (e.g., interactive whiteboards). Bearing in mind the fact that all materials in teacher education can be used in a variety of ways and for diverse goals, we can stipulate that this specific representation implies two things; firstly, that teaching can be viewed as a set of competences which can be studied and acquired in isolation and, secondly, that student teachers should emulate these practices and learn through copying. (p. 476)

She goes on to argue that editing may work to underplay the complexity of the classroom and the eclectic practices of teachers in terms of methodology. Furthermore, Hüttner reasons that while this editing may be time-efficient, it reduces the opportunity to highlight skills, such as 'classroom management, giving feedback and creating affordances of learning', which only become apparent during longer stretches of student activity. Pre-service teaching is a context where competency-based education is usually in operation, because there is some form of teacher accreditation involved, with a requisite set of benchmarks or criteria. When used as part of a competency-based approach, a published video might be shown to exemplify specific aspects of language teaching which can be helpful and illustrative to a novice, but it can also lead to language teaching appearing to be a set of isolated moves that the viewer should be emulating in their own practice.

While published videos in pre-service teacher education have tended to focus on discrete elements of 'ideal' practice (e.g., Harmer, 2015; Scrivener, 2011; Thaler, 2012), as these resources go into third and fourth editions they are moving to a focus on more varied classrooms (see Holliday, 2015), although they still tend to present a somewhat 'slick' representation of teaching and also often focus on the teacher-led elements of the class such as giving instructions. The focus for publishers is understandably on quality and usability, and their advantages often lie In better sound quality and higher-quality editing.

One of the problems that internationally published resources have is that teachers from one context might find video-recorded in a far-away context too far from their classroom realities. Cullen (1991) was one of the first to make an argument for local video materials rather than 'best practice' international resources. Local materials will feature teachers that are more relevant 'role models' than teachers from other contexts. Mann et al. (2019) found that these types of video resources are still being used in pre-service teacher education contexts, but the balance is shifting to watching resources built up by the institution itself (e.g., video banks or platforms) or individual trainers as well as an increased use of ad hoc resources (such as YouTube and Vimeo). These locally produced video materials can then be selected for their representation of local realities (e.g., large classes, low English levels, lack of technology) that many trainees face, and therefore feel more authentic and believable. Taking the above into account, it is undoubtedly a good idea to vary the kind of video input and video processes.

Reflective Break

1. In your pre-service teacher education programme, did you watch video of classroom teaching? How locally relevant was the video you viewed? What was your experience as a teacher-learner watching these videos?

2. If you are a teacher educator or teacher trainer, what type of video materials would you love to have to share with student teachers in your programme? Why do you think this video would be beneficial in their learning? What areas of practice do you find particularly hard for pre-service teachers to see modelled?

THE PRACTICUM AS CONTEXT

Video can help in the sequencing and staging of practice elements throughout the whole practicum programme and has a role in building language and pedagogic awareness, as well as socializing teachers. Further, Zeichner (2010) argues that, generally, research shows that there is some consensus around the following findings: (1) practicum experiences are appearing earlier and more often in teacher education programs than in the past; (2) these experiences are typically viewed by students as the most important part of their preparation; (3) practicum experiences are sometimes (if not often) found to be in contradiction to the methods and approaches advocated in university courses; and (4) practicum experiences tend to socialize pre-service teachers into the status quo for classroom teaching practices. Zeichner notes that video can help the practicum to be a 'practice-based model' that emphasizes 'participation, engagement, and reflection' (p. 342).

If we consider the priorities of the practicum, Darling-Hammond and Baratz-Snowden (2007) suggested that effective practicums include: (1) clear and explicit goals regarding teacher candidates' practice; (2) associate teachers who model sound practice; (3) regular teaching opportunities with ongoing feedback; (4) regular opportunities to apply theory to practice; (5) a gradual increase of teacher candidate responsibility in all areas of classroom practice; and (6) regular and structured opportunities for reflection on classroom practice. Video can help with all these priorities. In particular, it can aid with documentation around the teaching practicum, where it can help to make 'can do' statements more visible and concrete. This can also be helpful for benchmarking and accreditation.

In addition, it is important for teacher educators to be resourceful and innovative in phasing different elements of the programme. Kaya and Dikilitaş (2019) used observation, in-person classroom and video-based, of teacher practices combined with narratives and written reflective interviews. These enabled them to gain a deeper understanding of the process of identity development. The observations were carried out both by classroom visits and video enhanced observations. The evidence suggests that such a systematic approach is welcomed by the student teachers. One student teacher talks about his experience:

> At university, we have special Panopto cameras which I can observe myself or the lesson itself right after the lessons. If you ask me, I like them as they act like observers. Thanks to them, I could watch my lessons and focus on specific parts in the lesson and I could take some notes about the lesson. They are also helpful for self-reflection and seeing what you have done correctly or wrongly actually play a crucial part in your development as a teacher. (Kaya & Dikilitaş, 2019, p. 76)

Pre-service education works best when all of steps lead up towards a full-scale practicum. This is likely to be more effective if it follows this gradual introduction of classroom-related elements and goals. In other words, in demonstrating and connecting with school/teaching practice, it is better to have separate smaller stages (e.g., school observational visits or shadowing, video viewing) that build up to the full version of practicum (see Barahona, 2019). Video viewing can be an important addition to a phased sequence of initial exposure, observation, shadowing, teacher apprenticeship, micro-teaching, small group teaching, and fuller periods of teaching practice.

Video viewing is an experience in its own right. Wallace made the important distinction between received knowledge and experiential knowledge. A successful pre-service teacher education programme needs to strive for such a balance of 'received knowledge' and more 'experiential knowledge' and reflection (Wallace & Bau, 1991). Video is something that teachers can experience and talk about in more active tangible ways than they can when discussing generalized, or received knowledge (Goldman et al., 2007). In teacher learning, both received and experiential knowledge are important, and video can provide a tool for discussion and mediation of these different kinds of knowledge.

It is also important to foreground the importance of collaboration in teacher education—from the earliest stages of the programme through the practicum – and video has a role in fostering useful collaboration. This can mean working collaboratively with other student teachers (in micro-teaching, joint-planning, lesson study, peer observation, and feedback) but it can also mean making the most of contact with and feedback from college- or university-based supervisors and school-based mentors. Using video observation of classrooms can help teachers to work collaboratively, for instance when they view a classroom event and discuss it jointly. We recommend setting reflective video tasks regularly. Whole lessons do not need to be watched at one sitting; indeed, shorter is usually better for more focused observation. Collaboratively watching videos of classrooms can also help bridge the gap between the course and the practicum experience (Santagata & Guarino, 2011). In the early stages, micro-teaching using video can be a good way to prepare pre-service teachers before the practicum in a collaborative and reflective way (Mann et al., 2019). Bacova et al. (2016) focus on the value and possibilities of videoed micro-teaching, highlighting how the use of videoed micro-teaching extracts delivered by trainee teachers improved '[their] skills in teaching and learning, self-assessment and reflective practice' (p. 2).

It is the responsibility of those providing feedback to teachers on the practicum to present concepts in a way that makes sense to teachers. Video clips of classroom events have a unique role in making concepts concrete and accessible. Tripp and Rich (2012) share this practicum teacher feedback, 'Without video, I might have just gone the whole semester not really focused on anything specific and just kind of taught and tried to get better at teaching in general, but not really able to change anything specific' (p. 733). Video has an important role in providing detail from classrooms and supports written reflective practice, which has been criticized for a lack of detail when teachers describe and analyse teaching experiences.

Video also offers an important role in having a varied approach to developing observation and classroom awareness. This might include self-observation, stimulated recall, critical incidents, use of portfolios, use of observation frameworks, and tools (e.g., the self-evaluation of teacher talk, blogs, cooperative development, narrative inquiry, video, understanding staffroom talk, and critical friendships). Such tools can help mediate the theory (concepts, frameworks, models, and other input) provided by the teacher education programme.

Reflective Break

1. What are the unique challenges facing teacher education students entering or in their practicum experience? How do you think video analysis can help?
2. Which other elements/tools/apps/frameworks do you think can complement video materials in initial teacher education programmes? How would you use them if you are a teacher trainer/educator?
3. Look back at when you were a student teacher. How could video have supported your teaching practice in your early years/career?

CERTIFICATE, INSET, AND MASTER'S PROGRAMME CONTEXTS

In TESOL certificate contexts, such as the CELTA (Certificate in Teaching English to Speakers of Other Languages) from Cambridge Assessment, extensive hours of classroom observation are required. In this context, practical constraints sometimes mean that video viewing is the only way to 'make up' the observation demands of CELTA, and video recordings provide some variety and flexibility.

Partly it's been a response to the practical demands of being able to set up a sufficient number of hours of live observation and, as we are not a language school, and we are able to make use of classes at UEA (University of East Anglia) only insofar as they're available and appropriate. But it's only when the CELTA courses happen to coincide with courses that NILE (Norwich Institute of Language Education) is running concurrently where there are more opportunities for live observation. But at times of the year when that doesn't happen to be the case, then being able to supplement with video recordings is a very useful solution, and, as I say fortunately Cambridge (Cambridge Assessment) have relaxed that live observation requirement to enable us to do that. (ViLTE, 2019, Pulverness interview summary, accessed on 18/02/2022, https://warwick.ac.uk/fac/soc/al/research/vilte/ resources/interview_summaries/alan_pulverness_-_interview_ summary.pdf)

Particularly with COVID-19, it has been important to allow more video-based observation and Cambridge Assessment have allowed for more video-based observation hours. Gakonga (2019) provides a useful summary of the way in which video can be used in short, pre-service, teacher-training courses such as CELTA. She shares her experience and that of other trainers in centres she has visited in her capacity as an examiner in the following vignette, which summarizes the potential for video to be used to good effect in all stages of pre-service courses such as CELTA, including preparation beforehand, input on the course and to support teaching practice.

Vignette: Video in a CELTA Programme
Jo Gakonga
University of Warwick and Freelance Teacher Trainer

Pre-CELTA
CELTA is very intensive, and the majority of the course is necessarily devoted to teaching methodology. There is little time to consider knowledge about language and much of this is assumed. Although candidates' knowledge is tested in pre-course tasks, a lack of familiarity with the nomenclature of grammar is common, especially among first language speakers of English, and so video-based courses such as 'Grammar for Language Teachers' at www.elt-training.com can provide support and are often recommended by centres. Reading lists of appropriate books (e.g., *Grammar for Language Teachers* by Martin Parrott) are also usually given, but feedback on video-based courses suggests that it is perceived as more personal, accessible, and motivating.

During the Course
Video Use in Input
Video is helpful in input sessions to illustrate classroom practice with extracts used to show a range of classroom management techniques, examples of language presentation, different practice activities, and how to manage visual information in the classroom. This has the potential advantage of showcasing a range of different contexts, especially when discussing specific areas of language teaching such as young learners, teaching business, teaching advanced

or beginner learners, etc. A wide variety of practice is available on YouTube but vetting for appropriate quality can be time-consuming.

Video can also be used to add variety to input sessions. Some trainers report that short video-based presentations within input sessions are welcomed by trainees in what is a very intensive training course. The advantage of this is a change of pace (a chance to sit back, watch and take notes for a short time) and the ability of the trainees to review the video presentation at a later time if it is embedded on the course virtual learning environment (VLE). Trainers may produce their own video material or use freely available videos such as the CELTA Toolkit at www.elt-training.com.

In addition to using screencast video presentation within input sessions, some centres use a flipped classroom approach, giving trainees short video presentations (5 to 10 minutes long) to watch before the input session, which allows more time for practice in class. Flipped content works particularly well for sessions such as concept checking questions, lesson frameworks, and lesson planning, where concepts are introduced which may be new and which require support with practical application.

During Teaching Practice
Six hours of lesson observation is a mandated part of CELTA, and this may include watching the tutor teach the teaching practice class, observation of other teachers in the centre or video-based observation, with the latter having significant advantages. Using video material ensures that the trainer can accurately anticipate what the trainees will see, example lesson plans can be provided, and observation tasks can be given which focus on particular aspects of the lesson. Using a video-based observation also allows a lesson to be watched as a group, providing an opportunity for pauses for thought and discussion of practice. This is more time-consuming than a simple lesson observation but has the potential to be a valuable learning experience and provides the opportunity to refer back to these observations in other input sessions or in teaching practice feedback. As with the use of video in input, there is a challenge in sourcing good-quality recordings of lessons and the danger is that in edited classroom videos, learner to learner interaction parts are often truncated, giving an unrealistically teacher-centred picture of the lesson.

For Self-observation and Reflection
Self-observation of teaching practice is rarely comfortable, but it has immense value. Improved technology with recording possible on mobile devices, as well as the ease of recording online classes in Zoom or Teams, enables trainees to review their lessons and to use these for reflections in future lessons, or for their Lessons from the Classroom assignment. Challenges to this are that trainees

are often reluctant to watch their videos back and finding the time to watch the whole lesson may present a barrier. Solutions to this can include giving trainees a task to do whilst watching, but another productive path is to focus on shorter parts of the lesson that are captured by peers, and over the past two years I have been working with using WhatsApp and other online tools to enable trainees in a teaching practice group to do this. Online chat between observers during lessons is successful for many reasons, enabling a better understanding of the lessons to emerge and in addition to text chat, the conversation can also include images taken of the class and very short video clips. These may include instructions, concept checking, critical incidents within the class, etc. and will usually be only 10–20 seconds long. These can be viewed after the lesson by the trainee and also used during feedback to illustrate positive aspects to the lesson as well as areas for development. This length of video reduces the barrier to watching and re-watching and serves as a powerful tool for stimulated recall.

As teachers gain more expertise, their ability to 'see' more in lesson videos increases. Reflective practice is a skill that develops over time, and there is a clear link between the ability to notice and analyse observed practice and teacher experience level. Research into teacher cognition (Borg, 2015) and teacher expertise (Tsui, 2009) shows that the specific knowledge and teaching processes applied by expert teachers are sophisticated, professionally specific, and directly influential in the learning affordances provided by such teachers. In essence, what has been noted is that expert teachers have a better developed 'professional vision' (Sherin & van Es, 2009) than novices. This is one reason why expert or experienced teachers talking about their practice, ideally edited into footage of their classrooms, can be a particularly valuable resource (Mann et al., 2019).

Dragas (2019), talking about video use on an MA programme at Durham University, shows how video can help in building a longer-term sense of growth and development. They employ a systematic approach to the use of video in an MA-level programme that supports ongoing reflection on a particular module (see also Thompson & Kosiorek, 2017). Hüttner (2019) has also integrated video in a teacher education project at the MA level at the University of Southampton. She presents a detailed account of how video resources can foster teacher learning and provides guidance on how video can be used effectively as a resource for the development of a 'professional vision' on an MA programme. She is also the producer of the web-based resource VELTE (Videos in English Language Teacher Education). The VELTE resource (http://www.southampton.ac.uk/velte) is a free online resource that features full-length recordings of English language lessons, accompanied by a reflective commentary of the teachers featured.

Reflective Break

1. The following extract is taken from a discussion by three MA students with prior teaching experience. They have been using the VELTE resource (http://www.southampton.ac.uk/velte). They have viewed a lesson taught for upper-intermediate learners, focusing on the topic of fear. What do you notice about the students' conversation?

S6: one thing that I noticed that happened at different moments in the classroom it was that the teacher was trying to link the content (in hand) to the students' personal lives (.) even the [...] activities they carried out was mostly about their lives and minute thirteen he asks them 'is there anything you are afraid (of) if so why' and he asks 'do you know anybody who has phobia' it happened again in the minutes of forty-five he said 'do you like to be hypnotized by this man' I think one good way to learn vocabulary and for students to remember then it's (linking) them to [...]

S4: I noticed that when he [..] offered the story about the cable car [...] the students were fascinated to listen to that and really wanted to know, but they weren't so eager to divulge their own their own stories [...]

S3: don't you think that because he didn't allow extended enough extended time for example when he asked about if one of them has a situation when he felt afraid or [...] so I think the time wasn't very wasn't enough for them to answer because maybe they feel shy because it's about phobia and about real life so, and then he moved to the imagination so imagine that blah blah blah so yeah I think it wasn't enough time for them

2. What can be done to make novice teachers feel more comfortable watching themselves in video? How can teacher educators support them?

Hüttner uses this extract to show 'the professional vision of the students' as the teachers focus on what they noticed and how they interpret it. They are also able to offer alternative interpretations of the same event. We can see how the video makes it possible to be specific about what has happened and when (e.g., 'and minute thirteen he asks them') and also enables them to focus on student contributions ('but they weren't so eager'). There are positive evaluations of the teacher's behaviour (especially in terms of personalizing teaching), and there are also critical views (appropriate wait time/appropriate question). Whether teacher education students are in the certificate, pre-service, in-service, or Master's-level context, video analysis clearly can play an important role in their emerging understanding of classroom dynamics and their own practice.

SITUATING LEARNING IN CONTEXT WITH VIDEO CASES

Video cases provide useful authentic and concrete insights into teachers' beliefs, offer a portal into viewing methodology as it is truly enacted, and provide rich opportunities for scenario-based and inquiry-focused teacher learning, especially for pre-service teachers. Case studies also enable discussion of a full, context-based scene where viewers of the case can observe and comment on both teachers and classrooms as a facilitated group. One of the most important reasons to use video cases is that they help a programme become more practice-oriented, something that teachers consistently value. They do not have to be only examples of 'best practice' but can also focus on challenges and more 'grey areas' and puzzles.

Video cases can also help teachers imagine the nature of their future professional lives (Bayram, 2012) as they bridge the theory-practice divide and can even help to mitigate teacher shock and burnout at later stages of their careers (Farrell, 2013). Constructivist teacher education prioritizes practical and contextual knowledge in a continuously evolving way (Clark & Lampert, 1986) and video cases help teachers to focus on context and observable practice. This focusing process encourages the development of praxis (Edge, 2011) and greater confidence in novice teachers. Praxis as a term embodies a more reflexive relationship between practice and theory. At the very least, video cases can help pre-service teachers acquire well-grounded theoretical knowledge (Darling-Hammond & Bransford, 2005).

Vignette: Video in a CELTA Programme
Blanka Pawlak
Teacher Trainer at For English's Sake, Poland

Putting One's Own Teaching Forward
During a recent teacher training I was facilitating, I used two videos of my own teaching. In one video I showed a class in which I had tried to do my best using high standards of effective practices. In the second, I purposely used methods like translation, overusing L1, and more coursebook-oriented tasks than speaking.

I decided to use my videos as I see that for many teachers it's very hard to be observed. I believe it's necessary to get used to being observed, but through baby steps, not a revolution. The activities we carried out while viewing the videos were very focused.

After watching each video, we spoke about methods, classroom management, CCQs (concept checking questions), clarity of instructions, and more. We observed how the students in the classes appeared to react (you really see people's faces – it's super clear on the recording!).

> Subsequently, the teachers later had to implement their observations and ideas during their teaching sessions, which were also observed by all trainers and trainees. I got the feedback that our initial brainstorming with my two videos had been eye-opening and now they run classes with more confidence as well as are more prepared for what they might be looking at when reviewing their videos.

Rather than providing an overarching theory, guided analysis of video cases encourages a process of noticing and awareness-raising. Such guided noticing builds the kind of awareness of praxis that Edge (2011) values and the next quote is a great example of such a process. Here, Akcan (2010) provides an example of a novice teacher's report where the teacher is engaged in such a process of recalling, describing, and reflecting on a teaching incident (here, reflecting on appropriate levels of silence in the classroom):

> While they (students) were answering the questions, there was a great silence in the classroom- um, a silence not ordinary for a language classroom. I gave them 10 minutes to read the text and answer the questions; during the lesson, I thought that it was normal; but while I was watching the video I saw that the silence period was too long. Besides, I realized that I was so quiet during the lesson; it would have been better if I had been more active and energetic. (p. 40)

The early use of case studies was dominated by accounts in written text form (see Blijleven, 2005; Goldman et al., 2007). With developments in technology, new instructional possibilities and new ways of presenting, video cases have grown in popularity. Blomberg et al. (2014) provide a number of reasons why video cases are particularly valuable for pre-service teachers. In similar arguments to those we presented in Chapter 1, they argue that video conveys real-time complexity and subtlety of classroom teaching. Goldman et al. (2007) also argue that written descriptions or transcripts cannot achieve such richness and immediacy. Essentially, video cases can provide a 'fly on the wall' or second-hand experience of teaching (Miller & Zhou, 2007). One of the obvious benefits is that the novice teacher can be immersed in a classroom without the pressure of having to interact or make decisions and so they are better able to arrive at a concrete idea of what teaching entails (Brouwer, 2007).

Video cases can be divided into those from other teachers and those recorded by the teacher themselves. The former certainly provides the basis for discussion and reflection. If they focus on 'other' teachers, as we stated above, they can raise awareness of how an experienced teacher deals with their context and challenges (Kurz et al., 2005). Another advantage of 'other teacher' videos is that teachers are more likely to be objective and less emotionally involved (Rosaen et al., 2008). However, those recorded by the teacher themselves are important for the teacher to develop reflections on their own practice but also form the basis of a record of progress and development. Together with a tutor or mentor, the videos can encourage the discussion of progress and future professional development trajectory (Admiraal et al., 2014). They might be integrated into an e-portfolio that can serve as valuable documentation for future employment. It is important to say that video cases can be based on role-play or micro-teaching as well as real classrooms (see Koc, 2011 for useful examples).

Reflective Break

1. Video cases can either focus on teachers talking about their teaching or clips of classroom practice (or a combination of the two). What do you think are the main advantages of the use of video cases for pre-service teachers?
2. To what extent do video cases enhance initial teacher education programmes?
3. The general view is that video cases from the teacher's own context (or a similar one) are preferable. However, can you think of possible reasons why video cases from further afield might also be useful?

In considering the ways that video might be integrated into a course, module, or programme, there are some obvious starting points. For example, it is inevitable that we should consider the medium, duration, level, and needs of teachers. Seeking out videos from local teachers, in local schools, teaching local populations of learners is another way to craft more contextually sensitive learning experiences with video, as teachers are more readily able to accept the methods and approaches they see being implemented in familiar settings. Those who facilitate teacher learning with video will always benefit by being aware of the particularities of the context in which teachers will be working with video in order to best select appropriate video materials and set meaningful video analysis tasks.

Chapter 3

Video as a Process and a Material in Learning about Teaching

INTRODUCTION

In Chapter 1, we laid the foundation for *why* we employ video in teacher education, emphasizing that video processes and artefacts provide vital content to support teacher learning. In Chapter 2, we considered *who* engages with video in these contexts, namely teacher educators, along with pre- and in-service teachers. We noted that because teachers and their contexts vary in many ways, any teacher education process or initiative employing video needs to carefully consider the local needs, interests, and experience level of the teachers involved. Matching the use of video to the purpose of the programme is a complex enterprise for teacher educators, especially considering the wide variety of uses of video today.

In this chapter, we shift to *how* video might be utilized for such educational purposes. To this end, we highlight four approaches: videoconferencing, video production, screencasting, and the use of video repositories. These approaches can be used in any local ELT context, using minimal technology and free, open-access resources. What these approaches share is their potential for engaging teacher-learners and supporting their understanding of instruction and themselves as instructors, through the medium of video.

VIDEOCONFERENCING IN TEACHER DEVELOPMENT

Well before the Covid-19 pandemic, teachers around the world used Skype, Teams, Zoom, Google Meet, and other video communication tools, but videoconferencing has now become an important and ubiquitous element of teacher education programmes. It is often integrated into digital teacher education learning management platforms (e.g., Blackboard, Canvas, Moodle) that include multiple avenues for asynchronous communication, such as through blogs and discussion boards. These writing-based communication forms create opportunities for pre-service teachers' discussion, inquiry, feedback, and reflection in a social networking environment (Farr & Riordan, 2017), but videoconferencing offers unique affordances in teacher education that writing alone cannot. Videoconferencing has been employed in a variety of ways: to deliver instruction, conference with students, meet with distant colleagues, conduct, or attend in-house developmental workshops or consult with supervisors/mentors. Through videoconferencing, teacher educators can enable individualised trainer–trainee and peer collaboration within a fixed, local group as well as create the possibilities for much wider connections to other educators around the world (Ally et al., 2014; Carlson & Gadio, 2002).

Live video conferencing is especially helpful to novice teachers. A useful example comes from Benitt (2019), who describes an initiative using videoconferencing with pre-service teachers. This helped them 'to develop an analytical and exploratory stance on lesson planning, materials development and teaching techniques' (p. 121), through a collaborative process with a teacher of an English class in a German comprehensive school. The pre-service teachers cooperatively designed tasks and exercises informed by their knowledge of theoretical concepts and were able to evaluate them through discussion with the experienced teacher. The pre-service teachers considered videoconferencing a helpful tool in becoming more actively involved in a concrete teaching situation, and they also reported that they appreciated the opportunity to collaborate with an experienced teacher within a virtual community of practice.

In-service teachers can also greatly benefit from participating in a videoconferencing-based community of practice. For example, Alles et al. (2019) investigated the development of a learning community among teachers and a tutor during a one-year, video-based teacher professional development program, termed a 'Dialogic Video Cycle' (DVC). The study mapped changes in the teachers' discourse over the year of engagement and showed how conferencing via video on a regular basis created a sense of trust that allowed participants to discuss their teaching critically and to suggest various alternatives for each other's teaching.

Teachers can also benefit from videoconferencing as they support each other's research. The following vignette shows the value of regular reflective talk for teacher researchers, and also points to how the videoconference event can easily be captured and stored as a video artefact for subsequent examination. The ability to easily record and store live video conferences adds another dimension of their utility as a material.

Vignette: Video in a CELTA Programme
Claudia Bustos-Moraga and Maricarmen Gamero Mujica
University of Warwick

Video-Based Reflexivity: Cooperative Development While Doing a PhD
This vignette describes how videoconferences have gradually become a tool to enable intrapersonal reflexivity for our group of three PhD teacher researchers. This group was motivated by two main factors: first, as a response to the fleeting nature of spontaneous reflections (usually discussions were not recorded, and we only manage to save some bits and pieces once we are with a pen or a keyboard at hand). Second, we had been reading about Julian Edge's (1992) Cooperative Development and thought this might be helpful in sustaining focus and concentration on our emerging ideas (although we admittedly follow a very loose version of Edge's model). We had a personal and professional relationship, which became the foundation to generate a friendly space for cooperation and reflection through videoconferencing. These personal and professional aspects merge in our discussions and largely influence the decision of which sections of a session to record, if at all.

The use of videoconferencing and video recordings have become a key element of our discussions, although both are emergent aspects of our original plan. The occurrence of the Covid-19 pandemic began at the same time we had planned to start our 'live' meetings. As it has turned out, all of our encounters have been through videoconference. We began using WhatsApp video calls, but we soon realized that we wanted to record our interventions for later revision. We have used MS Teams since, which we access via our institutional accounts. The team's folder stores our videos and other documents we share or create depending on the sessions. It is hard to be sure whether we would have used videos, had the global situation been different. It is likely audio recordings would have been used instead, yet the fact remains that videos have allowed us to see ourselves on camera and share screens, thus enabling a level of intrapersonal reflection that audio alone cannot facilitate. We have been able to explore individually our own contributions to the group, the strategies we use to encourage each other's reflections, and the verbal and nonverbal cues we use to express our own research ideas and dilemmas to others.

The videos are stored in a private folder in Stream, an MS Teams built-in app. However, each participant may choose to download and later eliminate the recordings from the platform and keep them on their own devices for personal use, which has been mainly motivated by the ever-evolving nature of Teams and to avoid privacy breaches from external parties. Potentially, there can be up to three recordings per session, depending on who decides to record and what to record. At this stage, we only have a few videos, and we are still in the process of organizing them. Even though the recordings are available for the three members to watch, it is normally the 'recorder' who revisits her video, seeking to relive the discussion and remember comments made on the spot and prompt further reflections. The topics are not scripted, and we do not have a monthly agenda or similar planning; thus, each session includes whatever issue each one of us has decided to share either in advance or based on a last-minute decision. The core content provided by the videos are the oral interventions, as we do not include visual aids and we rarely share screens. However, the use of video recordings has enabled a type of intrapersonal as well as interpersonal dialogue that audio could not. First, by revisiting the videos of our interventions, the attention has not only been in the content (audio) but also in our facial expressions. These expressions not only have made the recalling of the reflection more vivid but also, have prompted discussions 'with ourselves' about why we said something and how we said it. Second, we have also used the MS Teams space to share videos of webinars about areas related to our discussions. Watching the videos has also deepened subsequent synchronous interpersonal reflections among the members of the group.

To summarize some of the ideas developed above, videoconferencing can provide the basis for collaborative and reflective work in a range of contexts. It can be helpful for relatively novice teachers in developing their confidence, awareness, motivation, and teacher identity. Working with more experienced teachers can be facilitated through videoconferencing too, enabling a concrete basis for sharing and supporting learning communities by video-recording and later reviewing and reflecting. It is important to highlight that recordings can be reviewed and reflected upon at a later time, which might give teachers more introspective time to gain insights of their own practice. In addition, as the vignette above demonstrates, teacher researchers can also use video conferencing for mutual support, generating the basis for data-led cooperation and reflection.

Reflective Break
1. In what ways have you used videoconferencing prior to, during, and since the Covid-19 period? Has videoconferencing been more widely embraced in your teacher education context?
2. What are possibilities you see in your context for greater or more strategic or systematic use of videoconferencing?
3. Which additional features (e.g., annotation tools, recording, chat box, chat box history, etc.) of Zoom (and other video conference platforms) could be used to foster reflection?
4. Are there any non-existing video conference features that you wished existed? Which ones and why?

PRODUCING VIDEOS IN TEACHER EDUCATION

The process and production of a video project offer an opportunity for teacher educators, student teachers, and language learners to express their understandings or to communicate messages multimodally. The design and production processes of video creation go well beyond text-only products, tapping into creativity, greater choice, and autonomy as students become the architects of their expression. Toci et al. (2015) share their experience in video production for teacher education and reinforce the centrality of the design phase as being a recursive process, noting that both faculty and teacher education students can produce videos that are useful for teacher education purposes.

One example of a teacher-produced video assignment for a teacher education programme is the Teacher Identity Project, which is publicly available as part of the University of Warwick ViLTE project (https://vilte.warwick.ac.uk/items/show/50). Here, the teacher educator invited student teachers to use video to 'identify their own funds of identity' (Villacañas de Castro, 2020, p. 25). The teachers made choices about what to include and brought together text, animations, still images, short videos, voice-over, and music to produce videos of less than five minutes. These are compelling artefacts for the teacher education classroom and promote authentic peer engagement in ways that go beyond sharing of simple text or speech.

Language learning students can also produce videos, or teachers can film students as they perform in classrooms. A series of such student presentations captured on video can be seen on Balbay's YouTube channel (https://www.youtube.com/user/seherbalbay/videos). These can offer course tutors authentic and targeted material to work with and talk about in class and may also be turned into rich material in teacher education contexts. Teacher Educators can highlight such possibilities of video production in modules on materials design and production.

Vlogging is another form of flexible and innovative video production that moves beyond reliance on written reflection (Liu, 2016). 'Vlog' stands for video blog and refers to a type of blog where most or all of the content is in a video format, and it involves creating a video of oneself where the video creator talks on a particular subject. Teachers can use vlogs to connect with other teachers (Mogallapu, 2011), to get feedback, engage in discussion and get advice by posting them on various platforms (e.g., TikTok, YouTube, Vimeo, Dailymotion, and Facebook). By using hashtags such as #teachingenglish, #englishteacher, teachers can engage others in discussion and commentary. Examples of a teacher using vlogging to share their action research publicly can be found at Dirk Lagerwaard's YouTube channel (https://www.youtube.com/channel/UCaRobWmFB_TLkqGM8Dg3IRQ/videos). Another motivation for making vlogs is the desire to multiply knowledge and

Mitos do Ensino do Inglês dos seus Filhos: 7

51 views

Figure 3.1. Screenshot of Vinicius Nobre's YouTube vlog: 7 learning English myths about your children (Nobre, 2018b)

to promote oneself (Nobre, 2018a). Vlogs are also used to create a bond with their audience (with teachers only, students only or both teachers and students). Notably, there are plenty of vlogs from teachers and trainers on social media websites (e.g. Facebook, Twitter, Instagram, TikTok) that show common conversation features: low tone of voice, 'chatty' lexical terms, use of anecdotes, hesitation, self-correction, and laughter. To illustrate, in Figure 3.1, Vinicius Nobre, a teacher trainer from Brazil, shares his expertise on the myths concerning children learning English (translated from Portuguese).

Vlogging has also been successfully used by teacher educators engaging their pre-service teachers in reflecting on their practice (Ong et al., 2020). In this case, pre-service teachers can create vlogs discussing their observations of their classroom, students, and mentor teacher and record their reflections on their teaching in field-work experiences. Essentially, the vlog functions the way journals do, but the ease of speaking rather than writing can make the process easier to accomplish on the run or to produce more extensive reflections than writing. The teacher educator can then 'read' the student teacher's body language, expression, and tone of voice to get a more nuanced take on how they are experiencing the programme.

The technical steps involved in producing videos has become relatively easy through the use of smartphones to capture video material and then importing clips directly into a video-editing application (e.g., iMovie). The imported video can be divided into clips, remixed, subtitled, and then shared through social networks. Once the video has been captured, learning how to move it to a computer and to store or share it is the next step so that the video file can be deleted from the recording device. When the video file is first downloaded from a camcorder or a portable digital device, it is generally too large a file to directly email or upload. For example, recording a lesson of 30–50 minutes can result in a very large video file. This

Table 3.1. Video-making tools and platforms

Moovly https://www.moovly.com/	Online platform to create explainer videos, promo videos, video tutorials, or training videos.
Explee https://explee.com/	Template-driven video creation and animation tool with a whiteboard style.
Canva	Customisable video creation and tool that allows users to collaborate in real time.
Animoto https://animoto.com/	Cloud-based video maker for educators, students, and administrators. It allows for one to quickly create introductions, recaps, educational videos, and slideshows.
Biteable https://biteable.com/	Web-based tool for slideshow and video creation with animated, live-action, or photo scenes in different styles and pre-made video templates.
Flexclip https://www.flexclip.com/	Online video and slideshow maker and editor. It allows cutting, trimming, and customising videos, or searching related pro clips for various editing.
Wave.Video https://wave.video/	Online video maker and video marketing platform that combines first-rate video hosting services, an online video editor, and an instant video landing page builder in one platform. This set of tools allows to create and repurpose videos for any channel.
Doodly https://www.doodly.com/	A software for the creation of doodle videos with a whiteboard, blackboard, or glass board style.
Powtoon https://www.powtoon.com/	A visual communication platform that gives the freedom to create professional and fully customised videos.
Squigl https://squiglit.com/	Content creation platform that transforms speech or text into animated videos with a whiteboard style.
Zoom https://zoom.us/	A video conference tool that allows users (hosts) to record their own video and save it on the cloud or their personal computers.
Thinglink https://www.thinglink.com/en-us/	An education platform used to make images, videos, and 360 content interactive with text, links, other images and videos, infographics, maps, or virtual tours in private mode.

is because video is usually recorded in 'high definition'. HD videos are measured at 1,920 × 1,080 pixels. The objective is to save the file so that it is closer to 'standard definition' – 1,280 × 720 pixels or 640 × 360 pixels. Standard definition is typically a size that works for uploading to online platforms. An HD video that runs for one minute will become a 100 MB file, but, if that same video were compressed down to a standard definition of 640 × 360, then one minute would be 10 MB. This is why compressing video files makes uploading and sharing much easier. There are free tools available to compress video, such as *Windows Live Movie Maker* and *iMovie*, which are built into PC and Mac operating systems, as well as others that can be accessed online such as WeVideo (https://www.wevideo.com/schools), PopcornMaker (https://popcorn.webmaker.org/) and Shotcut (http://www.shotcutapp.com/). There are also a number of open educational resource (OER) tools that can be used to create videos and we have provided some suggestions and details in Table 3.1.

Using these tools, teachers, and teacher educators can create videos for a variety of purposes. The videos can be varied and multimodal, incorporating both visuals and audio into the overall design. With Squigl (https://squiglit.com/what-is-squigl/) for example, audio can be generated from an uploaded script or voice recording, which then produces a drawing animation that matches this script. Different elements (PowerPoint slides, images, short animations, camera speaker recordings) are integrated into the final video material. Variety has been established as a key factor in maintaining teacher engagement (Mann et al., 2019).

Reflective Break

1. What types of video projects have you assigned students, and what were some of the challenges?
2. Looking at the list of video projects below (https://biteable.com/blog/creative-video-project-ideas-for-students/), which could be used with teachers for their learning, that could also give them practice with video production for application with English learner students?

   - **Create a book trailer:** Instead of a traditional book report, have students design a movie-style trailer that drums up excitement about a novel or a non-fiction book. Creating a book trailer gives students the opportunity to think creatively, share a story with their classmates, and reinforce their learning in a new way.

   - **Give a video tour:** To supplement the social studies curriculum, students can create a video showing off a significant location or their favourite part of the school. If you have a field trip planned, ask students to share their experience by recording videos throughout the day and adding voice-over narration. A video tour of the school is also a great way to share the campus with new students and visitors.

- **Recreate a moment in history:** Have your students research and recreate major moments in history. Videos help students visualize and remember these important moments. It also gives students the opportunity to experiment with digital storytelling.
- **Create a news channel:** To supplement learning in a current events class, have your students film a news broadcast covering both local and international events. Ask students to take on certain roles in the newsroom: anchor, sports reporter, weather reporter, or entertainment correspondent. Doing a news segment helps everyone get involved and promotes teamwork.
- **Start a portfolio:** Give students a chance to showcase what makes them unique. Art students can show off their best work and design skills. Students can create a video showcasing their community service and extracurriculars.
- **Promote a good cause:** Rather than writing a traditional essay or report, have students create a video advocating for a cause that is important to them. This helps students build their identities and develop persuasive skills.
- **Record and edit interviews:** Being able to conduct a good interview and edit it in a way that is appropriate for the purpose of the interview is a valuable skill in multiple industries.
- **Make a video self-assessment:** Grades are important. But being able to self-assess is also an incredibly valuable way for students to incrementally improve at any skill. Making video self-assessments gives students a more active role in the grading process and offers them a creative way to highlight the work they have put into a course. It also gives them a chance to make an argument for the grade they feel they deserve – a skill that easily correlates to performance reviews in their future workplace.
- **Film a job interview guide:** For most people, the interview is the most nerve-wracking part of getting a job. Creating a job interview how-to guide is a way for students to learn how to prepare for a job interview and help other students prepare at the same time.
- **Create a video presentation based on a written assignment:** Written assignments are the backbone of university education, however, the audience for most written assignments is limited to the professor and assistants. Creating presentation videos for their assignments gives students the opportunity to share their hard work with their fellow students, while also learning valuable video-editing skills.

SCREENCASTING IN TEACHING AND TEACHER EDUCATION

Screencasting is another form of video production, and there has been a growing use of screencasting in teaching and teacher education programmes (see Dawson et al., 2018; Stannard & Mann 2018; Stannard & Sallı, 2019). Screencasting involves creating a video of whatever is displayed on the computer screen, along with voice-over and possibly text, and it is used for on-screen tutorials, video lessons, presentations, and providing targeted feedback. Screen capture allows the user to record their voice and the screen at exactly the same time. This results in a video that can be directly shared or stored on a VLE (e.g., Moodle) or a channel (e.g., YouTube, Vimeo). There is evidence (see Stannard & Mann, 2018) that both language learners and student teachers appreciate the multimodal affordances of screencasting and the opportunity to pause and edit recordings.

From the teacher educator point of view, screencasting can be used for introducing a course or module, recording a lecture or webinar, flipped content, and providing a demonstration of a tool or app. Peachey (2015, p. 18) values the use of 'bite-sized screencasts' that can be 'a great source of continuing professional development' within a school or language centre. Many of the Massive Open Online Courses (MOOCs) that are produced by organizations such as Future Learn and Coursera also contain a lot of screencast videos. In teacher education, Stannard's site (www.teachertrainingvideos.com) offers a collection of screencast videos showing teachers how to incorporate technology in their teaching. In the case of teacher education programmes that are offered online, Stannard and Sallı (2019, p. 462) report that one 'real challenge in distance learning is the teacher presence and learners on these kinds of courses often feel a bit isolated' and can work through a module 'without really feeling their teacher's presence'. This is particularly the case where an online teacher-training course has lots of third-party materials from sources such as YouTube, Vimeo, and blog posts, and research evidence suggests that students expect to hear their teacher's voice on these types of courses and prefer it (Ladyshewsky, 2013). Screencasting can help deal with this by facilitating the production of content produced by the teacher trainer.

Outside of its use in online teacher education, screencasting has also been taken up by teacher educators in a variety of ways. Stannard and Sallı (2019) report its use for: (1) technical training so teachers can access information about systems and processes without the need for live sessions; (2) assignments in which teachers must create their own screencasts to demonstrate their technology skills; (3) informational modules to get multiple teacher trainers up to speed asynchronously; and (4) induction training for new hires in the teacher education context.

Another important use of screencast videos is found in giving feedback on assignments or tasks to language learners or to student teachers. The advantage of screencasting is that you can highlight the actual part of the text that you want to focus on (using a cursor and highlighting tools) and simultaneously use voice comments to provide feedback, as well as show teachers other sites and resources (websites and online tools). Research conducted by Stannard and Mann (2018) highlighted a number of benefits for teachers and teacher educators of using screencast videos, rather than written feedback which tends to consist of very short comments with little elaboration. First, they found that much more detailed feedback can be provided to trainees: A person speaks at around 140 words a minute and so in a 5-minute video, over 700 words of feedback can be provided as well as any visual information on the screen. Second, trainees find screencast videos clearer than written feedback because teacher trainers can provide more context when giving feedback and this helps trainees to understand the feedback better. Lastly, they found that trainees valued hearing the trainer's voice when receiving feedback. Thompson and Lee (2012) suggested that this might be to do with the use of hedging in the oral language, which softens the feedback, making it less threatening. For these reasons, they suggest that screencast video feedback may be more motivating than written feedback.

Reflective Break

1. Have you ever created a screencast video for teachers or English learners? What were the challenges and what were the benefits?
2. What kinds of screencasts do you think would be useful for your language learners (if you are a teacher) or for teachers (if you are a teacher educator)?
3. If you teach online asynchronous lessons, how could you assign screencasting tasks to your learners? Consider their level of familiarity with the technological tools that you have available for them.

VIDEO REPOSITORIES

The three approaches to integrating video in teacher education described so far: videoconferencing, video production, and screencasting, are all video-making processes as well as sources of video materials for teacher learning. This last approach, the use of video repositories, is about collating and organizing pre-made material (e.g., videos of classroom practice or teachers talking about their practice) that can be utilized to understand more about and prepare for teaching. Viewing these videos is an essential step prior to engaging in reflection of oneself or one's immediate peers via video. All too often, teacher educators jump directly into using videos of 'self' (i.e., asking teachers to reflect on their own teaching captured in videos) without laying the important groundwork of getting comfortable and skilled at observing teaching videos. Our view is that it is advisable to build up these reflective noticing skills with videos of others' video first. Steps to take in order to build such a foundation are described more fully in Chapter 4, but here we offer a review of video repositories and how they can be curated and videos selected to optimise the teacher learning experience.

A researched-informed approach to selecting videos for use in teacher education is based on considering the following five principles (taken from Hüttner, 2019; Zhang et al., 2011):

1. *Video cases from published resources should be grounded in a rich context.* A lack of contextual understanding of published video limits teachers' discussion. Teachers report learning more when they can ask questions of the teacher in the video and can be frustrated if they do not have access to the context around the published video. Such findings support Koc et al.'s (2009) suggestion of including the case teacher in the video discussion. When this is impossible, rich contextual information should be provided, including the teacher's instructional goals, student characteristics, lesson plans, samples of student work, what happens before and after the videotaped lesson, and the teacher's thinking behind significant events in the video.

2. *Video cases from published resources should be relevant to the viewing teachers.* Relevance appears to be an important factor that affects the usefulness of video cases from published resources. Therefore, when selecting a video from published resources, the grade level and subject topics should be close to the viewing teachers' own context and experiences. In other words, the context of the classroom in the video should not be too far removed from teachers' local ELT context, or they may dismiss the practices they view. Aspects such as classroom set-up, ethnicity of pupils and teachers, regional accents, and other features can either help viewers relate to the context or keep it at arm's length (Borko et al., 2008; Santagata & Yeh, 2014).

3. *Video cases from published resources should be as raw and unedited as possible.* Finding just the right video of ELT can be really challenging and time-consuming. While some websites may have some usable footage, the wide range of countries, grade levels, and purposes for ELT can make it difficult to find a good match using open-access resources. It is common to find much of the available video interlaced with advertisements, heavily edited and voiced over, with staged teaching. In these cases, the video can be more *about* teaching or advertising products or methods, rather than showing actual footage

of teaching. This is why in some cases purchasing video materials or producing one's own set of videos from local teachers makes more sense.

4. *Video cases from published resources should be curated based on learning goals.* When choosing a video to use with teachers, Peachey (2015) differentiates two approaches for selection: (1) select a clip that you think your students would be interested in, then analyse it and decide on the best way to exploit it with them or (2) decide what aim you would like to achieve and then try to find a clip that will help your students to realize that aim. He states that either approach is valid, though the first is generally easier to do. The content of the video material must be aligned with the learning tasks and goals for professional development. The teacher educator should reflect on appropriate questions: Is this a session on promoting group work in the ELT classroom? What kind of video will display this practice so viewers can discuss what they are seeing?

5. *Video cases from published resources do not have to be exemplars.* Hüttner (2019) classifies videos of teaching into four categories: standard practice, innovative practices, trainee practices, and representative practices. Best practice or exemplar videos have an important role (Ethell & McMeniman, 2000; Koc et al., 2009; Pianta et al., 2014) but it is also important to see routine classroom practice video as an object or stimulus for discussion. More important than finding a perfect model is being clear about the focus for the observation. For instance, does the video case incorporate the particular ELT focus that you wish to focus on in your professional development session? Does it contain the kind of ELT practices that you hope to promote in your context? More than video, audio quality can actually be the most important feature of highly useful ELT video materials. If participants are listening for feedback on form, for example, being able to clearly hear the teacher and student talk is essential.

These considerations are not exhaustive. Indeed, arguably, aside from the actual video choice, it is often the audio quality that can actually be the most important feature of highly useful ELT video materials.

Another key factor that will shape the selection of video, or how much of it is used is the length of the video material. The overwhelming finding from the ViLTE project (Mann et al., 2019) was that short clips work better than long ones, for a variety of reasons. Walsh (2020) also argues that relatively short 'snapshot' recordings have value in heightening awareness and deepening understanding. Sterrett et al. (2014, p. 273) report on the use of short video clips of teaching and learning in encouraging dialogue and collaboration where 'sharing teaching and learning via video clips allows for rich discussion in a safe environment' and allows for greater emphasis on 'reflection, collaboration, and growth'. Kiddle and Prince (2019) explain how video can allow input to be 'packaged into extremely short, dense and quite complex blocks because images and animations can show or demonstrate more in a shorter amount of time than text' (p. 119). Videos can be short because those watching them can make them 'longer' by re-watching the whole or sections, or by slowing them down to examine parts in more detail.

It is important to remember that video is a resource that can be used outside the synchronous training session. Setting teachers short video-based tasks and activities outside class, in the same way, that teacher educators routinely use supplementary reading, can create greater overall opportunities for access and engagement. Humphries and Clark (2021, p.1) provide solid evidence that students have 'a significant preference for chunk-style videos between 3 and 17 minutes in duration when compared to traditional long-view didactic lecture materials'. The chunk style also correlated with an increase in unique views (60%–67%), cumulative visits (54%–67%) and percentage completions (25%).

The following vignette provides an example of a video being used to showcase TESOL techniques and encourage reflection, without using a full lesson-length recording. In this case, the video is excerpted from a full lesson and is about 12 minutes in length.

Vignette: Using Short Video Cases in an MA TESOL Course
Yumiko Bendlin (Hunter College, City University of New York)

In this course, which is mostly delivered asynchronously in weekly modules, we are working with primary and secondary teachers to support them in designing curriculum and delivering instruction that includes a focus on language as well as on content. The course has more than 25 hours of fieldwork associated with it, but due to the varied settings in which teachers accomplish their fieldwork, it is impossible to really gauge what they are truly noticing or connecting in terms of the course content. The course is particularly focused on integrating content (history, mathematics, science, literature) with English language development goals. In our local schools, it can be hit or miss with being able to observe teaching that really showcases TESOL techniques used in content-based teaching situations. We want to make sure that all of the teacher candidates in the course are able to see basic strategies like building background knowledge, making content accessible, teaching in culturally responsive ways, and also setting a clear language objective that relates to the content being taught.

We decided that watching a lengthy video of a whole lesson might be too much for the teachers, and so we found a video from an alumnus of our program, which we edited to about 12 minutes in length. We then ask teachers to analyse the same video multiple times, each time with a different 'lens' or focus area. These include:

1. Discourse adaptations
2. Print modifications
3. Participation structures
4. Culturally responsive pedagogy
5. Vocabulary instruction
6. Grammar development

The video is housed in our learning management platform, Blackboard, and we used the 'quiz' feature in Blackboard to create an observation task for each of the six areas, using the same video and a dropdown checklist of TESOL teaching strategies that are all valid, but not all present in this particular video. Teacher candidates watch the video as many times as they would like and check off the strategies they believe are present. The 'correct' answers that were created by the course instructors appear once they have submitted their own responses, and thus it 'self-checks' and gives immediate feedback and explanations of the strategy and where it was occurring in the video.

Below is a sample of what students see looking at this video when we ask the teachers to focus on the culturally responsive practices visible in the clip. This is an area that is important to us in the program and much easier to talk about than to really see in action.

Instructions to Teachers
Please watch the video and check off the culturally responsive practices in the checklist you believe are visible in this clip. You will also be asked to write a short analysis of what you learned or noticed from this task.

Which of the following culturally responsive practices are visible in this clip? The teacher:

- knows home countries/languages of the English learners (Els)
- taps into background knowledge or makes links to students' lives and cultures
- brings in materials to build schema for topics likely unfamiliar to the Els
- encourages the use of students' L1 as a resource for content access
- anticipates ways problem-solving will be influenced by schooling in home country
- predicts how direct translation from L1 may interfere with understanding
- makes clear connections of content to students' lives and cultures

Figure 3.2. Still photo from video of teaching practice

- promotes the use of cognates
- correctly pronounces students' names
- posts artefacts and materials in the room or in lesson materials that make students' languages, cultures, or histories visible.

Afterwards, teachers write a reflection on what they gained from observing the video with the guidance of the observation checklist. We have used this task over many semesters and have found it to be one of the most appreciated and useful activities in the course. Teachers report that seeing the methods they have read about in action, in a local school and by a peer teacher encourages them to believe that they can also enact these practices. They appreciate being guided through the observation with the focused points to observe, and the chance the video affords them to debrief practice with their classmates and instructor in a much more focused way than they can do when they have not all witnessed the same lesson. Since these teachers go on in the subsequent semester to video their own practice, it normalises the process and helps them to see that no teaching is 'perfect' and they are not expected to put every method in the book into action.

In this vignette, a video is used first of another teacher, unknown to the viewers, to develop video analysis skills. For those who, wisely, wish to begin the process of looking at teaching via video of others rather than videos of self as a material, there is, fortunately, increasing availability of free online video (Mann et al., 2019). This video material is wide-ranging and includes case studies, classroom interaction, and teacher interviews. They can be found online in video-sharing websites such as YouTube or Vimeo (see Table 3.2 below for a list of suggested free, online repositories of teaching video). Some of these online video resources are 'one-offs', others are parts of online video-based learning websites, such as TeacherTube (https://www.teachertube.com/) or TeachingChannel (https://www.teachingchannel.org/home). Bates et al. (2016) show that these online repositories are usually themed into different sections, such as professional development, listening, and technology. Some sites are highly specialised, such as Interactive Teaching in Languages with Technology (iTILT) (http://www.itilt2.eu/pages/default.aspx), with videos of over 40 teachers in seven countries, all featuring how interactive whiteboards are used for language teaching. An open educational web resource was developed, which includes over 250 video clips of interactive whiteboard-mediated language teaching practice.

The following table provides websites that are possible sources for finding videos of teaching; none of the ten sample sites listed in Table 3.2 charge a fee. This list is annotated with brief information about the kinds of clips that can be found, the age or content area, ELT context, and any additional features that are notable about the collection. Within the collections, some are full-lesson length videos, but many are short clips, so length should be noted when choosing from these collections.

> **Reflective Break**
> 1. What do you think are the most valuable forms of video for pre-service versus in-service teachers?
> 2. What do you see as useful in your work in developing a professional video library of teaching? How might it benefit your colleagues?
> 3. What do you think would be important for you when selecting video materials to use when facilitating video analysis tasks?
> 4. Do you see the distinction of creating versus curating video helpful in creating a collection of videos you can use?
> 5. What are the advantages for learners to watch their teachers on video?

There is widespread agreement that video promotes teacher development as a material for reflection and teacher learning (Eröz-Tuğa, 2013). However, it needs appropriate support and robust systems to sustain it. This chapter has provided a range of different forms of video that might help foster reflection. As well as providing examples of video-making tools and platforms for both making and sharing video, we have also provided advice on websites that can help provide varied video content (see Table 3.2).

When considering how potent video of teaching can be in the teacher education context, we have argued that a systematic and sustainable approach to video use in language teacher development would benefit our field. Currently that is not the case, as many examples of good practice and resources are not shared, nor are they

Table 3.2. Sample list of sites with videos of ELT

Site address and overview	Grade level and context	Special features/ materials	Size of collection
https://www.teachingenglish.org.uk/teacher-development/video-tips *Video Tips* from the British Council is a series of short videos exploring different areas of teaching.	EFL at varied levels	Videos interweave interviews with teachers and classroom footage.	More than 20-but some have just teaching tips and do not have actual teaching footage.
https://www.britishcouncil.com.sn/en/programmes/education/english-connects/teacher-resources/supporting-secondary-efl-teachers-%E2%80%93-video *Supporting Secondary EFL Teachers: A Video Teacher Training Series (2021)* is designed for English teachers working with large classes in secondary schools in Sub Saharan Africa, consisting of a series of ten videos of model lessons filmed on location with selected local model teachers.	EFL at varied levels for teachers who manage large groups	There are downloadable supplementary activities for teachers who teach large classes in low-resource contexts.	10 videos
https://people.stanford.edu/claudeg/video/classroom-videos *Classroom Qualities for English Language Learners* at Stanford Graduate School of Education hosts videos of elementary-school English language learners during English language arts instruction as part of a research study.	ESL in U.S. public primary schools	An observation protocol linked to moments in the video collection	10 videos
http://www.teflvideos.com/ and https://www.youtube.com/user/BridgeTEFL/videos *TEFL Videos.com* provides access to videos that explain teaching practices and then interweave them with actual teaching footage demonstrating those practices.	Mostly adult ESL in the U.S., some EFL contexts	Also has how-to instructions on activity design and ability to purchase additional videos	5 free videos, with option to purchase membership and access more than a hundred

(Continued)

Table 3.2. (*Continued*)

Site address and overview	Grade level and context	Special features/ materials	Size of collection
https://www.elt-training.com/path-player?courseid=celta-toolkit&unit=celta-toolkit_1515518357181_0Unit CELTA training videos which have been curated by Jo Gakonga on her training site, https://www.elt-training.com.	EFL at varied levels	Embedded within a site that provides several teacher-training modules	6 videos
https://americanenglish.state.gov/resources/language-teaching-methods *Language Teaching Methods* is a video-based teacher-training series with videos showing examples of six language teaching methods that have been used over the past few decades: the Audio-lingual Method, Community Language Learning, the Comprehension Approach (TPR), Suggestopedia, the Silent Way, and the Communicative Approach. The project was produced by the U.S. Information Agency in 1990.	Adult ESL in U.S.	Has an accompanying teacher-training guide	6 videos
https://americanenglish.state.gov/resources/shaping-way-we-teach-english-successful-practices-around-world *Shaping the Way We Teach English* is a teacher-training course consisting of 14 video-based modules. Each module is a short video segment with examples from classrooms and educators around the world.	Young learners through Adult ESL/EFL	At https://blogs.uoregon.edu/aeiprojects/oelc/shaping/ viewing guides and transcripts accompany these videos.	14 videos, each with various short clips embedded into the teacher-training video
https://www.youtube.com/c/JohnHughesELT John Hughes is a well-known teacher trainer and materials writer who shares *practical* tips on ELT approaches and activities to be done in the classroom.	ESL and EFL at all levels	Most videos are captioned and relevant links to each video are provided.	More than 40 videos

https://sandymillin.wordpress.com/2017/11/11/lessons-you-can-watch-online/ 'Lessons you can watch online' is a collection of ESL and EFL short videos collected into this WordPress site.	ESL and EFL at all levels, including very young learners, trainee teachers and even an online teaching lesson on video	Sandy Millin provides a brief line about each video to aid in selection.	More than 85 videos
http://mnliteracy.org/classroomvideos Minnesota Adult Basic Education video collection provides a large collection of classroom and training videos focused on adults at the early literacy level.	Adult ESL in the U.S.	Videos are accompanied by viewing guides and curriculum links.	More than 75 videos
https://www.newamericanhorizons.org/ New American Horizons' *Teaching ESL to Adults: Classroom Approaches in Action* is a series of 12 videos.	Adult ESL in the U.S.	Videos are full-length lessons.	12 videos
http://www.shaping.lingvograd.ru/ The material consists of several sections and edited clips of 18 lessons. Of the 18 clips, one has been selected through which to initially explore several key ELT issues. The expectation is that once the viewers are accustomed to the 'pedagogy of questions' approach, they will develop questions themselves for the other lessons.	Primary through adult EFL in Russia	Several videos at the middle school level	18 videos

made readily available. While there are good-quality published video packages that may be purchased (a list of these can be viewed at https://warwick.ac.uk/fac/soc/al/research/vilte/resources/vilte_-_books_with_videos_v2.pdf), there is not yet enough freely accessible video. Video resources get published or are used within a project and then become unavailable (Mann et al., 2019). Significant investment is made in video resources for a particular project (funded by institutions or aid organizations) and then they are not obtainable (either because the project finishes or because OER permissions were not sought at the time of making them). This leaves a particular challenge for teacher educators:

> Teacher education programmes (both INSET and PRESET) need to make better efforts to aggregate and curate video resources to achieve wider access. This could be through databases of video (both classroom practice and teachers talking about their practice) but finding appropriate material can be challenging and video-based websites that support teacher learning should have searchable repositories of lesson videos (with titles, tags and visible metadata for each video) to help users identify and search for videos on specific topics. Supportive materials that clarify, situate, or extend each video such as transcripts and contextual information would also add value (see Forest & Mercier, 2011). If video and associated annotations can be stored in a 'multimedia container' then associated metadata such as tags, captions, subtitles, labels, links, data about gaze and proxemics will be more readily accessible for collaborative analysis and discussion. (Mann et al., 2019, p. 22)

There needs to be progress made both in terms of sustainability and getting permission to share beyond projects (through OER and Creative Commons). Pea and Lindgren (2008, p. 355) make a strong argument for more 'video collaboratories' where researchers 'work together to share datasets, tools, coding systems, analyses and other resources in order to advance the collective understanding of behaviours such as learning and teaching interactions that are captured in digital video records'. We believe that language teacher education will become stronger if we can make our practice more systematic and sustainable so that video resources and effective ways of working with them are more widely available and integrated.

Chapter 4

Learning to Look Descriptively at Teaching through Video

INTRODUCTION

In Chapter 3, we discussed *how* to obtain usable video footage, whether that video is of self or other. The technical and logistical hurdles of finding, sharing, and storing video might have initially seemed to be the greatest hindrance in getting started, but once you do have video in hand, what quickly becomes obvious is that the true challenge in using video to advance teacher learning is the often-overlooked fact that teachers are seldom trained in classroom observation and need guidance in *what* to do with video. Without explicit training in classroom observation, and when presented with video to analyse, our tendency is to jump quickly to conclusions, judgements, and recommendations about improving practice. After watching less than 60 seconds of video, most of us have already formed an evaluation and determined that what we are seeing either 'works' or 'needs improvement', effectively shutting off the descriptive analysis needed before evaluations might or should be made.

In this chapter, we will review some of the main reasons we want to explicitly develop non-judgemental observation techniques that support descriptive looking at ELT classrooms via video – namely bias and blinders. We offer several strategies for what a scaffolded approach can look like, offering a stepwise approach to clarify implementation. Employing these descriptive noticing strategies leads to more effective video analysis, guiding teachers to start with learning to observe objects like classroom photos, student work, or audio non-evaluatively before engaging in a review of video. Within this chapter, we present several tasks that could be used with teachers to set the stage for further descriptive noticing of video materials.

CAREFUL OBSERVATION AS A
FOUNDATION OF REFLECTION

Teachers engage in reflective practice with a sense of trust that it will lead to improved student learning outcomes. They engage in reflection-in-action during the lesson, reflection-on-action after the lesson, and reflection-for-action when planning (Farrell, 2013; Grushka et al., 2005; Schön, 1983). The teacher educator or trainer can support teacher reflection by helping teachers see the connections between student learning (their behaviours, their work products, their oral responses) to teaching (our plans, our materials, our responses, our behaviours). Hattie's (2012) work on 'visible learning' is helpful and important, as it reinforces the ultimate purpose for our reflection – to positively impact student learning – as well as underscoring the need for evidence to support our observations.

> A key premise is that [teachers] ask themselves about the effect that they are having on student learning. Fundamentally, the most powerful way of thinking about a teacher's role is for teachers to see themselves as evaluators of their effects on students. Teachers need to use evidence-based methods to inform, change, and sustain these evaluation beliefs about their effect. It is critical that the teaching and the learning are visible...The teacher must know when learning is occurring or not, know when to experiment and when learn from the experience, learn to monitor, seek and give feedback, and learn when to provide alternative learning strategies when other strategies are not working. (pp. 14–15)

How do we make teaching and learning visible? Artefacts such as student work samples, photos of classrooms, transcripts of teacher and student talk, and videos of teaching are materials that offer us the opportunity to engage in evidence-based reflection, especially when skilfully facilitated (Baecher, 2019). This offers teachers and observers a way to simultaneously and even collaboratively observe, as the events of teaching are accessible and viewable. Vygotsky's 'mediating object' gives name to this triangulated cognitive event, as seen in Figure 4.1.

In the mediation triangle, the addition of a third point (the record of the lesson itself, or the student work sample) reduces impressionistic interpretation of classroom events. This fundamentally shifts the reflection itself and elevates it from indirect observation and memory to a higher level of cognition. This shift happens because the mediating material 'is qualitatively different (constituting conceptual thinking) from non-mediated behaviour' (Chappell, 2014, p. 157). In other words, if there were no object, reflection would not be mediated. It would be unfiltered

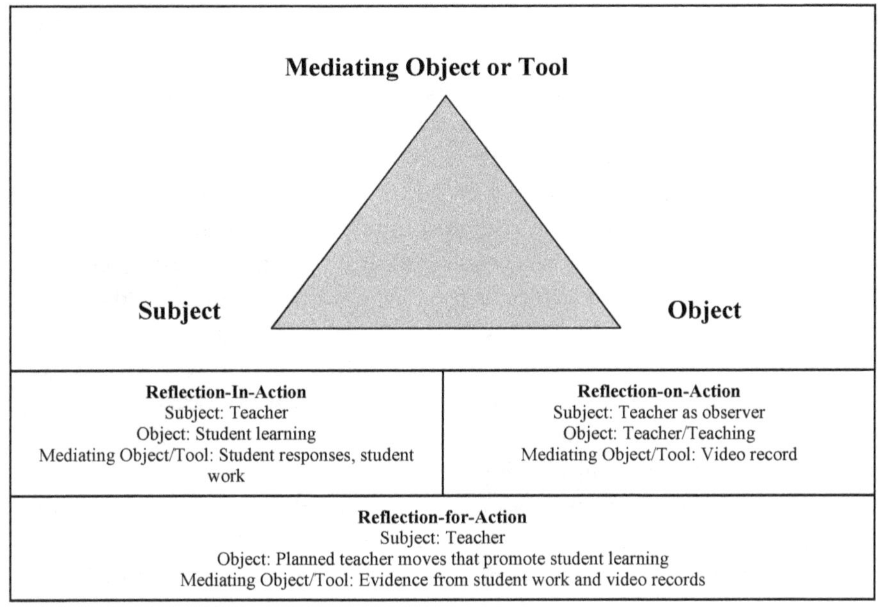

Figure 4.1. Video as mediating object

through anything beyond the individual's perspective, experiences, or point of view, in essence rendering it an act of argumentation. By introducing a concrete object like a student work sample, discussion and analysis is mediated and must work though this 'object as reference point'. This object then is the heart of evidence-driven dialogue and functionally changes what is possible in the reflective event.

However, the introduction of the mediating object (the video, the student performance) is necessary, but not sufficient, to drive evidence-based reflection. Too often, teachers are asked to immediately jump into observing video, which is incredibly dense as input to analyse, and they are also asked to look at their own teaching on video too early on. It is especially hard not to revert to judgement when presented with our own performance, so facilitators should always build up to that slowly and methodically. It is important to remember that while teachers are the objects of countless observations, very rarely have they participated in the type of training-to-observe that their mentors, professors, or supervisors might have received. In learning to observe, techniques such as verbatim scripting, classroom mapping, tagging, and tallying are all ways to promote non-judgemental, descriptive note-taking. These micro-ethnographic techniques help us avoid jumping to conclusions too quickly, and instead lead us to describe just what we see in front of us and thus expand our capacity to explore and learn from the rich data that is classroom interaction.

Even armed with these techniques, however, we each notice and attend to different stimuli when we observe. This has to do with our biases, blinders perspectives, and our prior knowledge. It is valuable to stop and acknowledge that no note-taking system can overcome our human predilections, and to keep them in mind so that they do not prevent us from systematic and careful observation. Indeed, having frank conversations about bias is essential before engaging in classroom observation. Otherwise, we run the risk that what we 'observe' is more of a projection of our beliefs and feelings than a reflection of the evidence. Many times, we are not even consciously aware of what our 'blinders' are (things that never catch or call our attention when observing teaching). *Project Implicit* at Harvard University has a variety of free self-assessment tools for teachers to engage in a discovery process about their implicit biases (https://implicit.harvard.edu/implicit/selectatest.html).

For instance, observers can be favourably or negatively biased towards what they see in a lesson, based on anything from their mood that day (Floman, et al., 2017) to their assumptions about the learners in the class. Observers' backgrounds and interests will also bias their noticing, for instance, if an observer really wants to see students doing extensive reading in every lesson and the observed lesson has none, the observer may react negatively to what is *not* there rather than sticking to observing what *is*. Whether the observation of teaching takes place in person or via video, addressing bias is an essential foundation for evidence-driven reflective practices.

> **Reflective Break**
> 1. What might some of the biggest challenges be when encouraging teachers to watch teaching descriptively versus evaluatively?
> 2. What types of bias and what 'blinders' on teaching practice are widespread in your teaching context? How might these influence what teachers in your context 'see' in video samples?
> 3. As a teacher educator or trainer, what are your 'blinders' or 'biases'? How do you consciously attend to them, either in terms of what you observe in a video of classroom practice, or in working with teachers doing so?

A SCAFFOLDED APPROACH: USING NON-VIDEO ARTEFACTS FOR DESCRIPTIVE OBSERVATION

In the section which follows, we present several types of tasks to engage teachers in the kinds of noticing and describing activities that lay the foundation for subsequent work reviewing videos of teaching and we focus on different ways of tuning teachers into descriptive discussion (rather than evaluative). These tasks scaffold the video observation experience and can be introduced before moving on to video analysis. We start with three examples of mediating objects that are *not* video of teaching as examples of the type of scaffolded steps to take to first increase participants' comfort level with descriptive observation, prior to engaging with video:

1. student work
2. photos of classrooms
3. audio records.

As discussed earlier, these can become the documentation of visible student learning through the teacher's process of making sense of them in relation to their pedagogy.

Sample Task: Analysing Student Work

One way to initiate the descriptive observation process is to use student work samples (writing or an audio or video of a speech) to have teachers engage in the mediation triangle (Figure 4.1). This reduces defensiveness as the instructional moves are not the mediating object and are only implied by the evidence presented in the student work product. The tuning protocol developed by the School Reform Initiative in the U.S. is a well-developed example that can be readily adapted for specific use in the ELT setting (https://schoolreforminitiative.org/doc/tuning. pdf). There are also videos of teachers engaging in this type of protocol that can be viewed to get an idea of the steps in the process (https://www.youtube.com/ watch?v=_hC--V6wTsU).

Step 1

Provide teachers a sample from a student's writing. A set which has been scored according to a rubric can be found here from Alberta, Canada: https://www. learnalberta.ca/content/eslapb/writing_samples.html.

Extract the sample without any scoring marks so teachers can form their own ideas:

> **Student writing sample (5th grade Level 3):**
> I one of the [Country A] people. I came to [Country B]. [Country B] was always spek English and French. In [Country A] was not always speak english or French it was different. There are no pets allowed in [Country A]. But here has pets. There is no snow, everything is green

but here snow and white. Here has Halloween and christmas but in [Country A] has no Halloween and christmas. In [Country B] I like the rules but in [Country A] there are too much rules. My house was small but here big.

Step 2

Ask teachers to mark up the student errors and create a list of linguistic features that they believe would be appropriate to teach next for this student. They can then share their thinking. This directs teachers to reflect-for-action, which minimizes the possibilities of judging and blaming the teacher and promotes a focus on the learner and learning.

Step 3

Ask teachers to imagine what the possible language objectives or activities were leading up to the production of this student work sample. This leads to a reflection-on-action perspective while being open to the many possible reasons teachers have for selecting particular goals or tasks. The process can emphasize the value of describing the actual student work as evidence rather than the teacher's actions.

Step 4

Teachers can then bring a sample of their own students' writing back to the group to repeat the process. After the group discusses the student's language use in the piece, the teacher can share their thinking and connect their beliefs and practices to the student work. This can again reinforce the complexity of observing teaching and learning and the importance of not making assumptions or determinations of what is 'good' or 'bad' but rather to use evidence to shape understanding.

Sample Task: Analysing Photos of Classrooms

Because classrooms are such complex environments, even a still photograph can be used to generate discussion that supports the development of observation skills that are descriptive rather than judgemental. Discussion of photos can be a chance to spot and address bias and how our backgrounds and preferences influence what we see, notice, and believe is important in classrooms. Like the student work samples, the material is 'once removed' from direct observations of teaching so it can slow down the rush to judgement and evaluation, praise, and suggestions that are typical initial responses.

Step 1: Purposely Trigger Bias

Provide teachers with some images of classrooms from around the world. Unfamiliar settings can trigger bias, personal beliefs, and judgements. Encourage teachers to be honest about what immediately comes to mind, and then assess which observations were pure descriptions and which were influenced by bias.

Some examples can be found at: Schools around the world – in pictures – World news (https://www.theguardian.com/world/gallery/2015/oct/02/schools-around-the-world-un-world-teachers-day-in-pictures).

Step 2

Ask teachers to notice any aspects of the physical environment, for instance in response to a checklist such as:

- Seating – how are the chairs positioned?
- Access – how does this allow for movement, learning, and conversation for ALL learners?
- Movement – how does the set-up promote access to materials or communicative tasks?
- Board – how are students seated in relation to the board?
- Materials – how are materials displayed to support language learning?
- Teacher's location – How does the teacher's location might influence the tasks?

Figure 4.2. Classroom environment. From Unsplash [Photograph], by NeONBRAND, 2017, Unsplash https://unsplash.com/photos/zFSo6bnZJTw.

Step 3

Teachers can then share their noticings. This directs teachers to reflect-on-action in terms of the elements of the environment that can be supportive of language learning, which is restricted to only what is visible in a single, still image. Teachers are generally amazed at how much they can see and consider even in a photo, which primes them to appreciate the complexity of classroom video footage.

Step 4

Teachers can then bring photos of their own classrooms back to the group to repeat the process. They can analyse one another's photos and brainstorm about how the physical environment can be shaped to promote language learning. Talking about photos of their classrooms may be less intimidating than having others look at their teaching as a first step towards video observation.

Sample Task: Analysing Audio Records

Video offers such rich visual input that sometimes our eyes overtake our ears. As language educators, however, audio can be even more important than video because it is a means to really attend to learner utterances as well as to teacher language. Audio is also particularly relevant to language teacher learning, in that our classroom talk constitutes teaching input. Research methods in our field, stemming from discourse analysis, have examined classroom talk via conversation analysis, where 'pedagogy and interaction are intertwined, in a mutually dependent relationship and we… examine the minute detail of the interaction to gain a full understanding of the instructed L2 learning process' (Jenks & Seedhouse, 2015, p. 6).

Again, like student work samples and photos, audio records can generate discussion that supports the development of observation skills that are descriptive rather than judgemental. Although the material can be considered direct observation of teaching – unlike student work samples and classroom photos – it still feels more indirect than watching video. Audio, like video, also offers the stop-rewind-replay opportunity and can be as surprising as video in terms of what it can reveal. For instance, programs like Teach*FX* (https://teachfx.com/) can automatically tally the amount of teacher talk versus student talk once the teacher has registered and recorded a sample of their own voice. Users can self-monitor and greatly change the amount of teacher talk in their lessons.

On her blog post, high school teacher Merdinger (2018) talks about the benefits she has gained from audio recording her own practice:

To evaluate student understanding, I can playback the recordings and based on student responses, determine the student's strengths and weaknesses. I use this insight to tweak my future lessons to meet student needs. I can also determine which students grasped the concepts the best or the worst, which helps me direct my attention in the days to come. Above all, recording class discussions has been the single most effective tool for self-reflection. I consider myself to be my toughest critic, and voice recordings give me many opportunities to improve my teaching and interaction with the students. I used to talk very fast and overuse buffers like 'um' and 'like', but voice recordings have helped me change that. Voice recordings has also helped me avoid long-winded, tangential 'side notes' during class discussion. I've learned a great deal about how I teach simply by listening to what I sound like while I am teaching… Whatever your goals may be, voice recordings will change the way you teach forever.

Step 1

Provide teachers with an audio sample from an ELT lesson. Isolate a segment of talk that can spark conversations about some universal patterns in classroom talk – such as the IRE (initiation-response-evaluation), teacher asking/answering own questions, teacher recasts – without telling teachers the focus.

Audio files from ELT classes can be produced in the local context or obtained from online sources. One way is to simply use available video of classrooms and only listen rather than view, such as ones available on YouTube: https://www.youtube.com/watch?v=MqLGBmr_oX0. YouTube videos are useful because later on, the transcripts can be downloaded and compared to teachers' transcriptions.

Step 2

Ask teachers to listen to a short segment (2–3 minutes) and transcribe what they hear. Usually, they will need it replayed a few times. They can then discuss what patterns they think they are noticing. The facilitator can provide the transcript as well. On YouTube, by clicking below the video file on the additional options menu, you can choose 'open transcript', which can then be copied/pasted into a Word document and printed out. By only hearing a small amount of talk from the lesson, analysis of the audio material stays in the arena of exploration rather than evaluation.

Step 3

Teachers can then bring an audio sample from their own classrooms back to the group to repeat the process. After the group discusses the classroom interaction heard in the audio record, teachers can share their thinking and connect their beliefs and practices to what was found in the analysis. This can again reinforce the complexity of observing teaching and learning and the importance of not making assumptions or determinations of what is 'good' or 'bad' but instead, using observation as a discovery mechanism to gain a truer picture of what is happening in a lesson.

Reflective Break

1. What are the opportunities in your context for introducing analysis of student work samples or photos before moving to video review?
2. How do you see descriptive observation of these non-video artefacts supporting eventual turning to look at video of teaching?
3. What are the benefits of using audio as a classroom observation tool?

A SCAFFOLDED APPROACH: BEGINNING WITH SHORT TASKS FOR DESCRIPTIVE VIDEO OBSERVATION

After you begin with non-video artefacts, you will likely create greater eagerness to explore video as an 'object'. After examining static objects like student work and images, and even audio, video will strike you as incredibly fast-moving, rich, and complex. At this point, very short clips and very focused viewing tasks will assist in the transfer of those descriptive observation skills for beginner observers (or seasoned ones who need to 'unlearn' highly evaluative observation practices). Another way to begin descriptive noticing using video is to focus on the language use in the classroom – rather than teaching moves per se. Walsh (2020, p. 21) recommends giving teachers 'a tool and focus' so that reflection becomes extremely 'do-able and useful'. He also argues that relatively short 'snapshot' recordings have value in 'heightening awareness and deepening understandings' of classroom interactional competence. We share three analytic approaches as examples of the type of scaffolded steps when beginning to analyse video.

1. selective verbatim note taking
2. mapping verbal flow
3. using time sampling.

Sample Task: Selective Verbatim Note Taking

Step 1

Provide teachers a very short clip (2–3 minutes) of English language teaching where the audio is clear. If you use one from YouTube, you can use the 'captioning' feature on the 2nd or 3rd review to assist in the process. For instance, this video can be cued up to minute 1:11: https://www.youtube.com/watch?v=g-KfTH9jY1k and note taking can occur for a set period, usually no more than 2–3 minutes. Teachers can be asked to write down, verbatim (exact word-for-word) all of: (1) the questions that they hear the teacher ask, (2) every moment of modelling the language, (3) every instance of corrective feedback, etc. Depending upon the instructional focus, videos can be chosen that are conducive for particular focused analyses.

Step 2

Ask teachers to selectively scribe only instances of the 'object' – instruction-giving, praise, correction, etc. They can then share their collected data back to the whole group. This directs teachers away from generalized notions and judgements about the lesson or the teaching and brings focus on the language moves in the video record.

Step 3

Ask teachers to imagine what the possible language objectives or activities might be in the lesson, or even the course philosophy or beliefs about students' and teacher's roles. This leads to a reflection-on-action perspective while being open to the many possible reasons teachers have for selecting particular goals or tasks. The process can emphasize the value of describing the actual instances of talk as evidence rather than the teacher's professed beliefs or actions.

Step 4

Teachers can then bring a sample of their own video back to the group to repeat the process. After the group discusses the language use in the analysed segment, the teacher can share their thinking and connect their beliefs and practices to their discoveries in these small focused samples.

Sample Task: Mapping Verbal Flow

Step 1

Provide teachers a medium-length clip (4–5 minutes) of English language teaching where the picture is clear and captures the whole class. Before watching, teachers could review some of the common seating configurations (https://www.tesolclass.com/classroom-management/classroom-seating-arrangements/) and types of grouping structures and consider how they might impact the flow of talk in an ELT lesson.

Step 2

Ask teachers to first view a video of a class for about 5 minutes with the sound turned off. They can sketch out a classroom map of the layout and set-up of the students and teachers and draw in some of the directional arrows for talk that they can see without hearing the audio.

Step 3

Turn the audio on and rewatch the same portion of video. Teachers can try to mark who is speaking and to whom. After comparing findings, discussion can be held as to how the verbal flow was related to the seating configuration, the task, or the teacher moves.

Step 4

Teachers can then bring a sample of their own video back to the group to repeat the process. After the group discusses the flow of talk in the analysed segment,

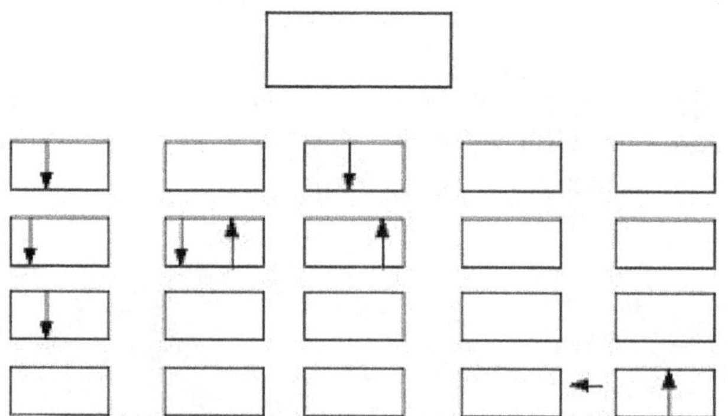

Figure 4.3. Classroom schematic to mark flow of talk

the teacher can share their thinking and noticing. Groups can generate alternative physical set-ups and task designs that could lead to different verbal flow outcomes that may be more in line with what the teacher looking for a communicative ELT classroom is seeking.

Sample Task: Using Time Sampling

Step 1

Provide teachers with a video that is a bit longer in duration – perhaps 20 minutes or so. Establish a focus for the observation – for example, promoting extensive reading during class lesson time. Using a graphic organizer to tally the results, teachers observe for the specific behaviour at established intervals, check a Y or N whether that behaviour is occurring, or count the number of instances where they see that behaviour is occurring.

For example, you will observe a 20-minute lesson whose focus is to note a particular student's reading behaviours.

Behaviour: Reading
Behaviour definition: Reading printed or digital material either silently or out loud.
Total observation session: 60 minutes.
Interval length: Indicate if the student is engaged in reading at 5-minute intervals.
Number of intervals: 10 in the 60-minute observation period.

Student name:	Interval number										Total # intervals
Date: Time:	1	2	3	4	5	6	7	8	9	10	behaviour observed
YES or NO											

Step 2

Tallying or marking are great ways to avoid judgement as much as possible, as long as the item is directly observable. For instance, trying to tally moments when students are 'engaged' will be tricky and lead to evaluation. After teachers have collected their data, they can see if they found the same results. Even with observation structures like time sampling, observers will wind up with different data. That itself can be revelatory.

Step 3

Teachers can then bring a sample of their own video back to the group to repeat the process. After the group discusses the findings in the analysed segment, the teacher can share their thinking and discoveries.

> **Reflective Break**
> 1. What are your prior experiences with any of these observation techniques: verbatim note-taking, mapping verbal flow, using time sampling?
> 2. How do you see these techniques supporting non-evaluative, more descriptive observation of video?
> 3. Which technique did you prefer and why?

PLATFORMS FOR ANNOTATING, TAGGING, AND TIMESTAMPING VIDEO

A growing number of researchers have established that video can help teachers gain closer understandings of the complex relationship between language, interaction, and learning (see Bozbıyık, 2017). It is particularly helpful for honing in on interactional features such as display questions, instructions, wait time, elicitation, feedback, error treatment, clarification requests, and teacher echo. In recent years, analysis of digital video has been enhanced with techniques like captioning, tagging, annotation, and timestamping.

One of the earliest video annotation tools, the Microsoft Research Annotation System (MRAS), enabled students to make notes (e.g., time-stamped annotations) on particular sections of a video that they perceived useful. Annotations are a useful way to pinpoint salient features of the video (Rich & Hannafin, 2009), offering an extra dimension to editing a video by reinforcing key messages and terms, and also make video resources more multimodal and interactive. Video annotation can have an important role as a tool for supporting teachers' reflective practices (Calvani et al., 2011).

Tagging video to make it interactive, of which annotation is one form, helps engage both teachers and learners. There are a number of tools that help you edit or embed tags. We would recommend a free tool such as ThingLink (https://www.thinglink.com/). Here you can upload a video (ThingLink accepts MP4, M4A, MOV formats) up to a limit of 2GB. After the video finishes uploading, you can then edit it. Thinglink has three buttons (add tag, settings, done) and a time bar so that you can choose where to add the tag. In other words, you can use the time bar to go to the time in the video where you want the tag to show. You then click 'add tag'. There are four kinds of tags:

1. Text and media tagging – This allows you to combine text, images, videos, links, and background audio (although most teachers create a tag with just text as this is the easiest).
2. Tagging content from another website – This allows you to create interactive experiences within the video scene. You can embed content from most web services if they provide an embed code. For example, you might embed videos from YouTube or FlipGrid (via a link).
3. Tour tagging – This tag takes the viewer away from the current image or video. It then goes to another ThingLink image, video, or 360 images. So, you can use the 'tour tag' to move from one creation to another.
4. Text label tag – This tag displays up to 100 symbols when hovered over. ThingLink crops and adapts images and videos to fit into tags.
5. Once you have saved the edits you've made to your tags, you can click the 'Done' button and then the 'Publish' button.

There are a number of other annotation tools to experiment with depending on your purpose. Videonotes allows teachers to paste notes in any YouTube video. The notes then become 'clickable' and return you to that part of the video. This can be a good tool for teacher educators to highlight and comment on particular sections of a video, especially focusing on classroom interaction. Videoant is another option that adds to the repertoire of asynchronous annotating tools available to the teacher educator.

Videopaper is a video annotation tool that integrates and synchronizes video, text, slides, and hyperlinks in one cohesive document. One possibility then is to ask teachers to use a video of classroom teaching and add captions, annotations, slides, notes in order to draw attention to features of the teaching, and also make connections with theories, models, and concepts from their training. Daniil (2013) explores how teachers used videopapers to reflect on their practice. The study found that a structured process of using videopapers supported the student teachers to engage in deeper types of reflection. Perhaps the main finding was that establishing a relationship between a text and the video engages with an in-depth exploration and analysis of their teaching practice.

The following table provides 10 suggestions for tools that can help with annotation and tagging video:

1. VideoAnt: https://ant.umn.edu/
2. ApowerEdit: https://www.apowersoft.com/
3. Edpuzzle: https://edpuzzle.com/

4.   PowerPoint from Microsoft Office
5.   Timelinely: https://www.timeline.ly/
6.   TurboNote: http://www.turbonote.co/
7.   Wave.Video: https://www.animatron.com/wave
8.   Renderforest: https://www.renderforest.com/
9.   Motionden: https://motionden.com/
10. Voicethread: https://voicethread.com/

These kinds of annotation tools can engage teachers in higher levels of reflections (making annotations directly onto videos). Kiddle and Prince (2019) talk about how their use of Edpuzzle (at the cheapest and simplest end of annotation tools) allows tutors to add questions to a video, which can be shared with students for work outside class or assigned to them as part of a course. They also talk about Voicethread which allows participants to interact with a video, add comments with text or video and annotate the images. This way participants can add questions, make suggestions, and compare their reactions and reflections to those of others. This can help establish a rich educational experience, with different layers of reactions and responses.

Annotation can also add value to the use of e-portfolios. One good example is the EU-funded project PREPARE (Promoting reflective practice in the training of teachers using e-portfolios) bespoke digital learning environment (PrepareCampus). This incorporated an e-portfolio application (Mahara) as well as an annotation platform for video analysis (edubreak®). The video platform encouraged novice teachers to watch and leave comments on their lessons. Timestamping enabled retrieval of particular incidents, and incidents allowed both self- and peer evaluation. Insights from the process were fed into 'longer-term assignments' (for more detail see Bauer et al., 2019, pp. 133–134).

For many teachers working with video, there is a trajectory of noticing specific interactional features, which leads to awareness-raising and then considering the significance of these all to the learning environment, something that Phan (2017, p. 63) summarizes: 'they were not only able to re-witness what and how they taught but also dig deeper into more understanding about their strength and weakness to improve their future lessons'. Kourieos (2016) and Dragas (2019) provide other examples showing how video can help focus on the details of classroom language.

Schwab's vignette below explains how a tool like VEO (Video Enhanced Observation https://www.veo-group.com/) can help with this interaction awareness-raising.

Vignette: Using VEO to Raise Interactional Awareness Among Future Teachers of English
Götz Schwab
University of Education, Karlsruhe

Context

The graduate course 'Understanding Classroom Interaction' was designed for prospective teachers of English at the primary and secondary level. It focuses on different theories of and approaches to better comprehend the role of interaction in Second Language Acquisition in institutional settings. The course work includes empirical considerations of how classroom research can be conducted and provides hands-on activities on dealing with interactional classroom endeavours. The latter part includes the intensive use of video recordings from a variety of contexts. Most of them are taken from a personal collection of authentic classroom recordings, though students are also given the opportunity to do their own micro recordings, provided they have access to a language classroom.

Process

In order to process the given data thoroughly, students receive an account for VEO which then is used for working online with an internet browser (https://veo.co.uk/). To start with, students get an introduction to the tool and the basic idea of tagging online as VEO in this case is used for tagging in retrospect. In the following session, course participants are asked to choose the SETT (Self-Evaluation of Teacher Talk; Walsh, 2011) tag-set which will be applied to one specific video recording – synchronously during class time or asynchronously at home. The results are then discussed in class before students are allowed to develop their own tag-set in groups of 3 to 4 students, based on specific issues either taken from the literature or their own teaching practice. This set can then be used on a different recording, again provided by the lecturer. Results of the tagging will be discussed within the group and then presented to the class.

    As an alternative, the mobile version of VEO could be used on an iPad when all students watch the same recording in class on a big screen and do the tagging simultaneously.

Evaluation

The use of an easy to use and accessible online tool has been very beneficial for students and teachers alike. The following comments – based on a survey after the course – may give an insight into students' perception of the tool:

> 'I think VEO is a great tool to analyse yourself as well as others in order to improve your teacher personality.'
>
> 'VEO is quite easy to use and thanks to the preset tag-sets [it] doesn't need a very long preparation time.'
>
> 'I think it's a great opportunity and really helpful to reflect on classroom interactions'
>
> 'Very intuitive, simple and helpful online tool for tagging videos. It can help to analyse problems in the classroom and find areas that might need to be improved.'
>
> 'I like online tools in general. I think this will be the future.'
>
> From a lecturer's perspective it should be added that the act of providing access to the tool for every student may take time but once this is achieved, VEO helps enormously to support reflection and raise interactional awareness among prospective language teachers.

One of the distinctive features of VEO is that new sets of tags can be developed (see also Sert, 2019). The value lies in the selection and tagging of sequences that can be shared with collaborating teachers or trainers, and comments can be included in annotation panes which sit next to the video clips (see also Batlle & Miller, 2017; Hidson, 2018; Körkkö et al., 2016). Tagging and timestamping features are particularly helpful in terms of relating teaching practice and classroom choices to students' learning behaviours and task outcomes.

Lightfoot (2019) highlights the value of platforms and tools in relation to teachers' sense of agency with working with video of teaching.

> Whether or not used in conjunction with F2F input, the use of technology can help to shift the power, control and agency to the teacher to make decisions about where to place their focus. For example, Iris Connect, Onvu Learning and others are working with schools and teachers to install video technology which can enable self-observation, reflection and developmental discussions with peers as well as mentors or supervisors. This shifts the power away from a single observer to the teacher and enables him/her to more easily reflect on his/her own practice. (p. 53)

Perhaps, for this reason, there is clearly a lot of interest and increasing use of video platforms and tools for both pre-service teachers and for professional development. A wide range of institutions (e.g., universities, Ministries of Education, British Council, International House, school districts) are increasingly using platforms and tools such as VEO, OnVu, Panopto, and IRIS Connect to record teaching to facilitate reflection and teacher development. VEO is being used to develop suitable tags and support for CELTA programmes, and IRIS Connect has been used in various contexts including high-resource contexts in the UK and more low-resource contexts such as Thailand (see Mann et al., 2020). There are also a number of studies that report on the use of IRIS Connect (https://www.irisconnect.com/uk/impact/research/). The value of these platforms is that classroom videos can be reviewed and commented upon by teachers.

With IRIS Connect, although videos can be stored and reviewed, one of the benefits of this system is that it enables live lesson observations as well. The system also allows the sharing of lessons with invited colleagues (i.e., each teacher can decide whether to share a video and who with). Teachers are using these tools (e.g., VEO and IRIS Connect) for peer observation, and they report that using the online web platform helps them to understand classroom decisions and choices. Such reflection on classroom practices leads to self-awareness and more concrete discussion (see Davies et al., 2017).

Platforms also provide more opportunities for teachers to connect and collaborate (Ally et al., 2014). These platforms can enable trainer–trainee and peer collaboration within a fixed group but also much wider connections to other educators around the world (Carlson & Gadio, 2002). Platforms include content and information (as well as videos) and increasingly can be accessed by mobile phones. Although there are still challenges in relation to internet speeds, mobile phones have functioned as an important 'leveller' in language teachers having access to these platforms and their videos, information, and resources for development (Ally et al., 2014; Weber et al., 2018). Some video platforms are free but sometimes they have limited functionality – however, for a one-off course, it is often possible to use a trial version. For instance, Ortega (in Mann et al., 2019, p. 58) explains how she uses Eduflow:

> I found Eduflow serendipitously. It was a new platform designed to host online courses. I was looking for a site where I could share video demonstrations for my participants, and also, where my participants were able to share self-captured videos only with other members of the course. I chose Eduflow because with a free account you can create up to three courses, and upload videos. But what I liked the most was the option to use the *flows* for participants to submit their work in video form recording from the webcam on their own devices eliminating the hassle of uploading heavy files or files in the wrong format.

Reflective Break
1. Which of the suggested activities seem most do-able for you and other teachers at your site?
2. Have you used any of these video annotation platforms, or simply used time-stamps or other ways to break down teaching on video into smaller components for analysis?
3. What challenges might teachers have when tagging their own videos using a video tool such as VEO? How can they overcome such challenges?

Chapter 5

Reflecting through Video: Self-Observation

INTRODUCTION

As discussed in Chapter 4, when a 'mediating object' is reviewed, such as a student work sample, a photo from the classroom, or a video, it allows the viewers to hold and share the moment, thereby supporting teacher reflection on and for future action. As teachers engage regularly with video reflection, they transfer that experience to their in-class teaching, becoming more able to reflect on events happening at the moment 'in practice' (Tripp & Rich, 2012, p. 679). Just like holding up a mirror provides information that compels us to adjust our perception of how we look, video challenges us to let go of what we wish we saw (in our mind's eye), and come to a clearer understanding of what is (what we see in the mirror). Once we experience that dissonance, we never look at our classrooms without asking ourselves what it is we are *not* seeing.

Observing teaching descriptively may feel awkward or difficult at first, as we prevent ourselves from rushing to judgement (our natural tendency). Using techniques like tallying, classroom mapping, and annotating support the viewer in slowing down and looking more intensively at particular aspects of classroom interaction. As teachers shift to looking at their own rather than others' practice, continued methodical, careful looking can help us see even more deeply and more extensively. In this chapter, we examine how video review of self connects to high-quality reflective practice and how individuals may proceed with self-examination of their teaching via video.

REFLECTING ON ONE'S OWN TEACHING THROUGH VIDEO

In previous chapters, we have noted numerous ways in which teacher reflection on their own practice can be fostered through video, especially when the process is carefully scaffolded. In Tripp and Rich's (2012) review of studies reporting the benefits of using video for teacher reflection, they applied the following six criteria to review the dimensions of video use included in their review: (1) type of reflection tasks, (2) the guiding or facilitation of reflection, (3) individual and collaborative reflection, (4) video length, (5) number of reflections, and (6) ways of measuring reflection. Overall, they found a great deal of variety in video reflection tasks, guiding frameworks and methods used to measure the benefits of video reflection, but all the studies they reviewed found positive impact on teacher reflection. These six criteria are helpful in organizing a systematic approach to bringing video into a teacher reflection process.

Mann and Walsh (2017) further point to several key features of video that particularly appear to link to teachers' depth of reflection, which should also be considered when designing teacher reflection activities with video. Table 5.1 provides a summary of their main points.

Reviewing teaching practice via self-captured and self-managed video affords teachers one means by which they can undertake focused reflective analysis of practice, both individually and within teacher communities (Hubber et al., 2019). Such videos can then become objects of discussion. So, for example, video can be used to open up discussion of both 'what happened' and 'what might have happened' – this is very different from using video as a model of what 'should' happen.

This is a key point for us. Video can be used to open up choices, options, and potential rather than as a visual cue of do's and don'ts. John Fanselow has been using video for many years to help teachers 'see' choices and this is an important part of this approach to helping teachers notice, discuss, and then make small changes in teaching (see Fanselow, 2018 for a recent statement of his core approach to using video). According to Whitcomb et al. (2009), video captures the richness and complexity of teaching events which foster a deliberate examination of classroom practice. This exploratory stance aligns with the concept of dialogic reflection. This means that reflection and articulation are co-constructed in relation to both people (e.g., dialogue/interaction) and artefacts (e.g., video extracts, transcripts etc.). Dialogic in this sense captures the interface and interaction between reflections, narratives, metaphors, past and present, video and text, model, and data. Just as dialogue is between people, reflection is furthered in the interface of video, reflection, data/evidence, tools, and affordances.

Video supports such a dialogic reflection because it encourages a concrete and focused approach. It enables pausing and repeated watching, each time through a different lens, and this in turn encourages more ownership and more focused analysis and reflection (Baecher & Kung, 2011; Tan & Towndrow, 2009). Importantly, it allows the exploration and articulation of connections, relations, dissonance,

Table 5.1. How video analysis connects to teacher reflection

Focusing on detail	Video encourages a focus on the concrete details and events of classroom practice, taking the trainee teacher back into a teaching moment, incident, choice, or decision. Helping novice teachers to locate specific aspects of their lessons makes the process of reflection more data-led.
Revisiting moments that were unnoticed while teaching	A teacher might use video to look again at a moment they were conscious of at the time, but video can also enable a focus on the 'aspects of classroom life that a teacher might not notice in the midst of carrying out a lesson' (Borko et al., 2008, p. 418).
Developing sensitivity to classroom talk	One of the challenges for teachers is developing sensitivity to classroom talk. For instance, it is often challenging for novice teachers to implement wait time, and video review can assist teachers in noticing who is responding to questions.
Making the abstract concrete	A video extract can provide a strong stimulus for discussion and associated reflective thought for viewers. Hiebert and Hollingsworth (2002) argue that the educational community lacks a shared language for describing aspects of teaching and that video has a particular role to play here. For example, key phrases such as 'problem-solving' or 'language experience' often mean different things to different teachers. Video of lessons therefore offer the possibility of pinning down aspects of classroom experience so that the teacher has a clearer frame of reference and can therefore be more specific about their own actions and intentions.
Mediating teacher noticing	Golombek (2011) talks about video as a tool in mediating teacher reflection in teacher-learner conversations. She shows how mediated use of video helps to reconstruct such a teaching event and to share intersubjectivity.
Supporting novice teacher's voice	Kurtoglu-Hooton (2010) presents evidence suggesting that greater integration of video observation into teacher-training contexts can give teacher candidates a greater voice in their post-observation conferences and supports novices' ability to analyse and understand their own practice rather than solely relying on a supervisor to do that for them.

contradictions, grey areas, and the potential or possible. One of the advantages of video is that it keeps things data-led and concrete, rather than having to rely on vague memories of the classroom event, which can lead to a potentially superficial and inaccurate account of events. As Hennessy (2011, p. 463) says, the use of video helps keep the focus on practice and 'address issues of practical relevance which are meaningful to practitioners as well as academic researchers'.

This dialogic effect can also happen in the space between teachers' espoused and their actual teaching practices. Revealing incongruence can create powerful leverage for change in reflective thinking and/or practice, and there is potential for video to establish the basis of an interface between what a teacher believes and what the evidence is (Rosaen et al., 2010).

VIDEO OBSERVATION OF SELF

As previously discussed, structured viewing tasks of other teachers (not oneself) are a great way to get teachers excited about the classroom as a learning lab, focus in on the 'small moments' that make up classroom interaction, and prevail against our tendency to quickly judge and critique. A descriptive rather than purely evaluative stance ideally transfers to our self-observation through video. As we strengthen our capacity to examine teaching and learning, we promote exploration of our own practice. Then we also avoid seeing observation as a ritualistic evaluation activity that we simply try to 'get through' as quickly as possible. This can lead to heightening teachers' motivation. In other words, the use of video for teachers' self-development can potentially empower them to analyse and celebrate their professional growth over time and enable them to compare themselves to themselves, thus giving them a sense of accomplishment and personal satisfaction (Nobre, 2018a).

Video serves as an important tool in this scaffolded approach. As visualized in Figure 5.1, it can empower our movement from observation of learners to observation of others' teaching, to observation of self, to others' observation of self. Ultimately, being observed by others – while a routine and important accountability and assessment component of teacher preparation, schools, and institutions – is limited in its developmental impact if teachers are not comfortable and skilled at observing teaching and learning.

Teachers' work with video of their own practice may take place in two ways:

- *individually*, for teachers to privately observe, reflect, and notice using video recordings from their own live classrooms or even from their teaching in distance-learning contexts.
- *in groups*, to build a professional vision for teaching and to foster collaboration and collegial interactions that use video records as a way to break down the classroom walls and promote peer intervisitation.

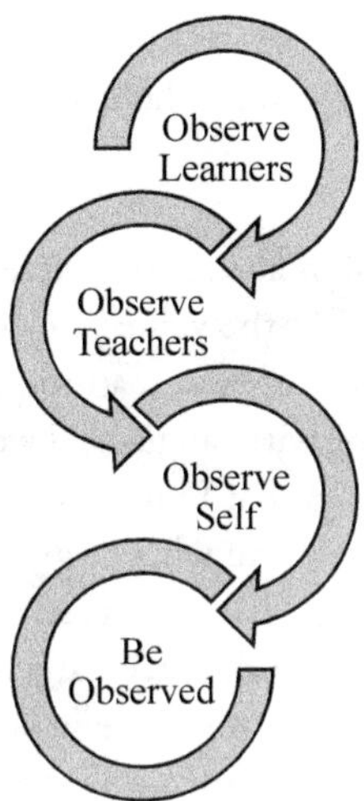

Figure 5.1. Scaffolding viewing of teaching: moving from other to self

In both of these uses for video, we want to re-emphasize the need for scaffolds that use the video material to its greatest advantage; that is, the rewind, pause, review, and replay of specific instances of classroom interactions rather than its use to make holistic judgements about a lesson or a teacher.

Often, even novices who first begin to review video of their practice as a part of their pre-service education programme are able to explore common dilemmas such as giving instructions, eliciting language and asking questions. The following data extract shows a student teacher grappling with her challenges in setting forth instructions and guiding questions during the lesson.

> While watching her own video, Esra realised that she had trouble with speaking in English. She observed that she would 'start a sentence with one structure and continue with another or say something at the end when [she was] supposed to say it at the beginning'. Her mixing of structures and sequences, especially when giving instructions, resulted in confusion among the students and diverted their attention from classwork. Similarly, Meltem noticed in her video that she paused too much while interacting with the students, and when she 'tried to construct the sentences spontaneously in the classroom, [she] wasn't successful, and the students realised it too'. She felt she lost the respect of the students as well as the control of the class due to the gaps in her speech and consequently decided to prepare her questions ahead of time. (Eröz-Tuğa, 2013, p. 179)

In the following example from Sarah (in Dragas, 2019, p. 145) we can see how video reviews feeds into a reflective log, where learning points and ideas for future actions emerge:

> Reflecting on our discussion about corrective feedback in a reflective session, my personal belief in the value of feedback has strengthened. I can see that I need to try to create an atmosphere where students feel comfortable experimenting with language. I would also like to improve my decision-making skills so that I know better when to provide feedback, how to do it effectively and what to give feedback on.
>
> On viewing the recording, I have observed that I made some attempts to monitor the students but didn't keep any records. This meant that the feedback I did do focused on content only, missing the point of the lesson. It also couldn't be heard by all the students. Consequently, my attempt was of negligible value. Reflecting on this, I identified a number of problems. Firstly, despite including feedback on the lesson plan, I didn't plan what to give feedback on and how to do it. Secondly, I didn't have the means to be able to collect information on language points. Finally, I failed to appreciate the importance of this part of the lesson and on the day, almost gave up.
>
> This led me to identify a number of planning solutions. From a lesson perspective, feedback needs to be given a more prominent place. For activities, a four-stage planning process (task aim, instructions, task and feedback) would ensure feedback is included. Finally, planning how to record evidence to feedback is essential. I was able to test these solutions on 8 December where I applied the four-stage planning model for the activity and ensured that I had paper with me to record language during the lesson. The result was positive, and I noticed a change in my own sense of self-efficacy, feeling more like a teacher.

As we can see, we can map a reflective trajectory that begins with a 'personal belief', goes through different reflective stages, and ends with concrete next steps, greater 'self-efficacy', subsequent action, and a feeling of being 'more like a teacher'. The novice teacher develops an increasingly sophisticated analysis of her own classroom practices by drawing on evidence from different data sources (video-recorded classroom interaction and self-reflective reports) collected over the academic year.

More experienced teachers, such as those completing the DELTA, also find great value in videoing their own classrooms as part of their ongoing professional development. Chinn shares examples of this in the ViLTE video collection (https://vilte.

warwick.ac.uk/items/show/13), and in the same collection, Sherif (https://vilte.warwick.ac.uk/items/show/10) highlights ways he exploited short micro-teaching videos for the professional development of his teacher trainees in Kazakhstan.

MICROETHNOGRAPHY IN SELF-OBSERVATION

The first step in scaffolding the process of self-observation is to isolate specific viewing targets, in order to delimit the range of possible features to observe. But how does a specific focus come to be selected? In general, a broader view is first taken in, and then particular aspects of a class become interesting to explore further. Copland and Creese (2015) parallel practices undertaken by field researchers that apply to classroom observation:

> In the field the ethnographic observation often starts with the researcher taking a wide-angled view. This might mean that the researcher visits and observes as much as possible, taking notes about the people, social spaces and social practices in the site under investigation (including virtual sites). However, as time goes on and participants' beliefs, values and actions become more apparent, the researcher will look more intensively and repetitively at an action, site, person, group, or routine and ritual, and these areas will become the focus of the field notes. (p. 40)

This close examination of small moments is the heart of *micro*ethnography and is linked to the use of video. Micro-ethnographic approaches involve studying 'how human realities are produced, activities are conducted, and sense is made, by inspecting video recordings of actual events frame by frame' (Streeck & Mehus, 2005, p. 382). Microethnography is also referred to as 'video-based ethnography' because it is so often used by researchers video-recording in natural social settings where people are interacting. 'These recordings are then analysed repeatedly and rigorously, with attention to both the participants' talk (who says what, when, and how) and their embodied behaviours (the relative location, movement, and orientation of people and things)' (LeBaron, 2008, p.1).

Video analysis is intrinsically tied to micro-ethnographic methods, as these require focusing on small moments of classroom interaction, using transcription, mapping, and describing rather than judging or evaluating. As described previously, observation that employs tallying, counting instances, or analysing snippets of classroom talk is an entry point to examine particular moments of teaching deeply.

Meticulous attention to moment-to-moment communication between students and teachers helps us to better understand how teachers and learners interact, and thus arrive at particular outcomes.

Video also visually provides more than just the language of the lesson, which can be captured in audio recordings and transcriptions. 'Working with videotaped interaction invites us to attend to what is going on visually and nonverbally, providing a corrective to the temptation to make analysis unduly logocentric. When people negotiate face to face, they put their bodies as well as their uttered words into play, and phenomena of gaze, posture, and movement, as well as use of artefacts and documents, contribute closely to unfolding courses of action. The organization of talk intersects with the organization of embodied action' (Glenn & Susskind, 2010, p. 122).

Due to the richness of the data-both visual and auditory, and the time needed to carefully employ micro-ethnographic observation techniques, teachers will work with video most efficiently by examining short clips from their lessons rather than trying out these close-looking observation techniques on a long video. One way to choose which smaller segment to review is by recalling those portions of the lesson teachers feel were problematic to return to those moments via their video review. These 'critical incidents' are 'recounts of specific classroom events and experiences such as incidents that teachers deem critical for their professional development' (Farrell, 2013, p. 109). Incidents could be simple occurrences (Angelides, 2001), yet what makes them critical is how they are conceived/interpreted by the teacher. Moreover, as critical incidents 'are flash-points that illuminate in an electrifying instant' (Woods, 1993, p. 357), they exert a substantial impact on teachers' present and future cognition and practices.

Sample Self-Observation Approach: Using a Critical Incident to Focus on Instructions in the ELT Classroom

In his blog post, Clements (2015) talks about receiving some feedback from a supervisor that suggested his instruction-giving could be strengthened. He agreed with his supervisor that at times he found himself repeating his instructions and students took a while to get started on tasks – but he felt unsure where to begin and unclear from the supervisor's generalized feedback, where he could adjust his practice. Using this experience as a critical incident, he first turned to some reading on the subject of instruction-giving. After reviewing Scrivener's (2012) criteria for effective instruction-giving, he developed his own shortlist of aspects to observe in his teaching:

Features:

- position in room when giving instructions
- complexity of language in the instructions
- amount of language in the instructions
- pace of delivering the instructions
- sequencing of the instructions
- signposting steps in the instructions.

Additional features could be added to this set of observables, such as:

- text support for oral instructions, on handout or board
- checking for understanding of instructions through student responses
- appropriateness of instructions – whether needed for task
- student need for repetition or additional support once task begins
- use of L1 or English during instruction-giving.

Clements then video-recorded several class sessions, focusing afterward on his instruction-giving and taking notes on what he was seeing. He writes of his self-observation process with video:

> It took me about 10–15 minutes to scribble down ideas after each class, meaning I had to choose classes where I had some free time afterwards... You could underpin your self-development task with a bit of research. Flick through a few books that talk about instructional techniques, or perhaps ask experienced colleagues for tips. Watch some videos online maybe. Attend a workshop on the topic if there's one coming up. You might not even need to refer to literature or get help to improve your technique, the answer might be intuitive... You keep it accurate by being honest. You keep it useful by making it focused. The good thing about this type of analysis is you start to recognise patterns. Imagine doing this over the course of 3 or 4 lessons – it can be a real confidence booster as you learn just as much about what you do well than what you need to improve on... If you're doing this for your own development then I thoroughly recommend filming yourself in action – it's more insightful than post-lesson evaluations.

Sample Self-Observation Approach: Using Rubrics/ Checklists to Focus on Questioning in the ELT Classroom

Most teachers are familiar with long checklists or detailed rubrics to evaluate their teaching in their workplace or teacher education contexts. For the developmental purpose of viewing one's own teaching, however, selecting just a few discrete aspects

	INSTRUCTIONAL ELEMENTS (The instructor did the following)	✓	**DEMONSTRATED ACTIVITIES** (Check all appropriate boxes below; fill in information at appropriate spaces)
INTRODUCTION	Provided review of previous work as warm-up exercise for students		Used an activity that fosters social communication
			Used an activity to review previous learning
			Used an activity to orient group to new topics
			Other:_______
	Stated lesson objectives and reviewed the agenda		Indicate observed activity:_______
	Provided opportunities for students to become familiar with lesson materials		Previewed vocabulary
			Used visuals to preview (e.g., table of contents, headings, graphic organizer)
	Checked students' background knowledge on the topic/lesson		Asked questions about the topic
			Engaged students in an activity (e.g., Jeopardy, word association)
			Other:_______
PRESENTATION	Used appropriate presentation style(s) for content and audience		Lecture Discussion Role play
			Demonstration Case study Other activity/game
			Other:_______
	Gave adequate/appropriate explanation of new concepts		Describe:_______
	Responded to students' questions		Answered questions immediately
			Deferred responding until later in the lesson
			Posted questions for later
	Periodically checked students' comprehension		Asked general questions (e.g., Is there anything you do not understand?)
			Asked content-specific questions
			Asked students to summarize in their own words
			Other:_______
PRACTICE	Set up practice activities clearly		Clearly modeled activities
			Gave clear oral and written instructions
			Gave examples and/or demonstrations
			Scaffolded learning
			Other:_______
	Gave practice activities during class		What was observed?_______
	Monitored/assisted all students (individually, paired, and grouped)		Listened to each group interacting
			Answered only clarifying questions
			Other:_______
	Used a variety of communicative strategies for practice of language skills and content		Students paired/grouped for speaking
			Students exchanged writing for targeted oral feedback
			Students prepared projects/posters, etc., and shared with class
			Other:_______
APPLICATION	Gave students time to apply what was learned		In a new situation during the lesson
			In their own situation after the lesson
	Gave students time to share their application (work)		Paired/grouped students
			Whole class
			Other:_______
	Gave students an opportunity to comment/evaluate each other's work, as appropriate		What was observed?_______
EVALUATION	Evaluated students' application of concepts		Used communicative activity
			Used a test
			Other:_______
	Gave students an opportunity to evaluate the lesson, as appropriate		Used written reflection
			Used oral feedback
			Other:_______
FOLLOW-UP	Gave students opportunities to review materials over time		Assigned homework
			Used warm-up/closing activity
			Used review games or discussion
			Other:_______
	Gave students opportunities to ask questions		Orally or in writing during class
			Posting electronically
			Other:_______
	Gave students a task to further investigate content		Assigned homework
			Linked with future lessons
			Other:_______
	OBSERVER'S COMMENTS:		

Used with permission from the Technical College System of Georgia, Office of Adult Education

Figure 5.2. Adult ESL observation of teaching rubric

can support more descriptive observing as in the approach Clements (2015) took in examining his instruction-giving practices. Using observation focus 'menus' can be a way to scaffold this process for teachers looking at their video, based on the literature in methods of ELT. For instance, we are all likely to have seen observation forms such as the one found here (https://files.eric.ed.gov/fulltext/ED505392.pdf), which was designed for use in adult English as a Second Language programmes in the United States.

Often, forms provide insight into the philosophical and theoretical stance towards effective ELT. By seeing what observable teacher moves are identified on the form, a vision of what constitutes desired practice emerges. There are always specific moves that are *not* captured on a form, but they can be a good place to begin a self-observation routine.

For instance, if the focus for the teacher is questioning techniques (as seen in Figure 5.2 in the 'Presentation' section), then specific items outlined on an observation form can be helpful for self-appraisal because they break that larger concept of 'questioning' down into smaller observable chunks. These could include observing who the teacher is calling on, wait time before choosing responders, how responders are chosen, how the teacher probes for more elaboration, etc.

Inside every aspect of teaching is a wide array of possible micro-moves. Being 'micro' means they are well-suited for being observed under a 'microscope'–that is, through video, as described earlier in reference to micro-ethnographic observation techniques.

Aspects of Teaching that are Well-suited for 'Micro' Observation Via Short Excerpts of Video

- *Questioning:* Who posed the questions? What was the cognitive demand of the questions?
- *Response opportunities:* Who gets called on? Where are they seated?
- *Praise:* What praise is given? Is it specific or general?
- *Feedback:* What attention is given to form(s)? Does the teacher recast or use other techniques?

Aspects of Teaching that are Well-suited for 'Macro' Observation Via On-site or Long Lengths of Video

- *Pacing:* What was the length of each lesson component?
- *Content accuracy:* What concept/content was presented and how did the students work with it?

- *Materials:* How did the students interact with materials across the tasks in the lesson?
- *Rapport:* What positive interactions occurred between students and between teacher and students in the lesson?

In the excerpt below, a student in a Master's TESOL program shares how using video helped her better understand her classroom management techniques regarding who is called on to respond during the lesson. She begins with a critical incident and connects that to an area of practice on her practicum rubric related to student participation.

> **Vignette: Using Video to Understand Classroom Management**
> *Ruth Oviedo Diaz (Long Island University-Hudson, USA)*
>
> Another thing that stood out to me was one student in particular who started calling out and talking in the lesson. This can be frustrating for students who are following along to what the teacher is saying and other students who have their hands raised patiently waiting to be called on. I wrote down the names of the students that I called on throughout the lesson. I found that 14 of the 23 students in the class participated in the discussion.
>
> I realized after watching the video that the number could have increased if some students didn't call out. I saw that as soon as a student called out an answer, hands immediately went down. This took away the opportunities of others to participate in the lesson. I also noticed that only 6 of the 12 English language learners (ELLs) spoke during the lesson. Most of the ELLs had their hands raised during low-stakes tasks and once they weren't chosen for those tasks the participation started diminishing.
>
> I need to train myself to call upon the students who are not jumping around in their seats and waving their hands. This is a surprisingly difficult task because the human eye is tempted to pay attention to obvious movements in the environment. So, a student calmly raising their hand will be noticed *after* the student who was jumping around and making noises. Now that I am aware of it, I will start to practise calling on the calm students during my lessons.
>
> I also need to think about my lesson the night before and identify the low-stakes tasks that I can call on more hesitant learners to do ahead of time. This last Friday I actually practised that in my lesson, and it was a huge success. I noticed that after the student completed the low-stakes task he was actually encouraged to keep participating because his confidence increased. This was a trend that I noticed in my other ELLs as well.

In this vignette, we see that she began with the more salient issue of a student who called out responses, but then as she began to explore the video, she noticed the impact of that calling out on other students and how she was contributing to that result, rather than ascribing it to the student. She realizes that questioning is not just a spontaneous interaction but can be improved through planning and intentionality as to who is given the opportunity to reply.

The following vignette also provides a good example of making video use around the practicum structured and reflective.

Vignette: Using Video Self-Reflection in Teacher Training
Richard Baldwin and Tobias Ruhtenberg
University of Borås, Sweden

Context
Examination tasks involving the use of video technology were introduced within a teacher-training programme at the University of Borås, Sweden in 2015. As part of their practicum in a Swedish school, pre-service students were required to choose one or more of their lessons to be video-recorded and then create a digital paper with embedded video.

Process
The process used was based on the application for video technology outlined by Brouwer (2011), where video technology is used as a trigger for reflection. Students were required to review and edit video footage to create a digital paper that included a total of about five minutes' embedded video, and which was to be published and uploaded to a teaching platform. Within the digital paper, the students were required to analyse and reflect on the chosen video sequences, connecting their text to the wider literature on teaching and learning as necessary. The students were then required to present their video paper and recordings orally to a small group of student teacher colleagues and a course teacher, as well as take part in an analysis and group discussion based on the contents of each of the papers.

Evaluation
The comments made by students within the video-embedded papers and in an online questionnaire show that the students were without exception positive to the idea of using video as a method of reflection. The findings are in line with those in previous studies, which have shown that video can help student teachers to reflect more deeply on their practice.

However, the relationship between text and video differed between students. Some students described seeing things in the video clips which they had not known about before and that the video clips had acted as a catalyst for reflection. Other students' reflections, however, did not have any clear connection to the clips chosen. The video clips included were mainly described in the text rather than reflected on.

The benefits of presenting their papers to other students, as well as the teacher trainer, in a follow-up session were taken up by many of the students. The feedback provided by classmates and teachers created new areas for reflection which they had been unable to see themselves. We conclude it to be important to discuss the contents of papers in small groups, which more often than not enable the discussions to take place at a higher conceptual level as well as bringing aspects of theory and practice closer together. As Kleinknech and Gröschner (2016) have noted, peer and expert comments can broaden pre-service teachers' self-reflection and help them to evaluate situations in a more balanced, analytical, and critical way.

Another issue is the amount of freedom given to students in deciding on the contents of their digital papers. In the examples discussed here, the participants were given complete freedom to decide on what issues they decided to reflect on in their papers. However, some of the participants in this study could have benefited from more support with the reflection process generally, in terms of both clearer instructions and/or scaffolding. As Sitzmann et al. (2010) have pointed out, self-reflection is a difficult and challenging process and student teachers probably need a clearer understanding of the performance question.

Most of this section has explored various pre-service and in-service contexts. Some of them are face to face and some of them are online. However, it is important to remember that the use of video is possible outside institutional training. Mann and Walsh (2017) use the term 'in the wild' to capture professional learning opportunities that happen outside formalized training. It captures the autonomous and more ad hoc opportunities that exist. The following is a good example of this where a teacher (Ipalibo-Osokolo, 2020, p. 47) used video as an entirely personal and autonomous way:

> Let me tell you one thing I discovered a few months ago. I thought to myself that sometimes instead of asking my colleague to observe my class, why do I not use my phone to record my class and then see how I perform. It is awkward watching your own video. Almost too embarrassing. The first time I did it I was quite surprised by how my

movement was, I think I walked too much in class, I was also too loud and did not really attend to my students' questions satisfactorily. After several attempts, watching and reflecting on my videos, I have understood that my practice was better than it was.

We think this is a powerful example of the simplicity of the idea. Wherever the context, a video recording can be the prompt for reflection and teacher learning. It can be done as an individual, a pair, or a group.

Reflective Break

1. Would you rather observe yourself in video using a more structured plan (e.g., using a checklist) or less structured? What do you see as the benefits or restrictions of each approach?

2. Watch the video by Chinn (https://vilte.warwick.ac.uk/items/show/13) featuring various DELTA trainees sharing their experiences of videoing their lessons. What skills did they develop by videoing their lessons?

3. Many teachers do not want to experience the discomfort of watching themselves on video. Video record a five-minute lesson. Decide on the focus of your observation and write a reflective note when you finish the lesson. Watch your videoed lesson and reflect on these questions:

   (a) How did you feel while watching yourself on video? Was it as uncomfortable as you thought?

   (b) What did you learn from observing yourself via video?

   (c) Would you recommend this self-observation to other teachers? Why or why not?

4. What are the main challenges or fears that teachers might face before and while videoing themselves teaching? How can they overcome such challenges?

Chapter 6

Video Observation with Peers

INTRODUCTION

The review of one's teaching via video records ideally occurs after a carefully staged series of steps, moving from looking at short clips of the teaching of others with structured viewing protocols, and after some foundational work in learning to observe descriptively has occurred. We presented these ideas across Chapters 4 and 5, and now we turn to the rich possibilities of sharing one's video of teaching with others for discussion, analysis, and reflection. Again, we emphasize that teachers should not begin looking at their own teaching via video for the first time in front of peers or supervisors. Respecting teachers' vulnerability is paramount as well as ensuring the peer group has clearly defined procedures in order to make the process focused, growth-oriented, strengths-based, and descriptive rather than only evaluative.

Sharing video with a colleague or a group of educators, when led by a skilled facilitator, is transformative professional learning. In this chapter, we begin by framing the research on using video in peer reflection, especially as part of creating a shared vision of practice, and then provide several concrete strategies for approaching a peer-review process. We conclude with an example of how both self- and peer observation can be combined to fuel institutional-level change.

DEVELOPING A SHARED PROFESSIONAL VISION

Mann and Walsh (2017) establish the importance of collaboration in pushing reflective practice beyond an essentially individual pursuit. They detail how teacher education can encourage a collaborative view of teaching, one where peers/colleagues support and scaffold reflective practice and where teachers are not restricted to isolated teaching roles but see belonging to networks and communities of practice as viable and essential to their development. Tsui (2009, p. 30) argues that teachers find 'sharing reflective writings and engaging in collaborative reflections' particularly useful and such collaboration can be fostered with video-based activities.

It is helpful, before considering video-based observation with peers, to first recall the ways peer observation is already implemented and align those with the addition of video to the process. There are a number of well-known benefits to visiting peers' classrooms, and video review can extend the opportunities of peer observation, as seen in Table 6.1.

When teachers have experienced a transmission style of education, they may not be used to drawing on and referring to their own experience in explicit ways and this might need support. They might also need support in working towards collaborative ways of working that video-based peer development requires. Collaboration with colleagues is increasingly an important dimension of teaching, and being comfortable with the rhythms and challenges of teamwork is an important dimension of independent professionalism where teaching is too often seen as an isolated and individual pursuit (Kiely & Davis, 2010). High-quality video-based peer observation draws on the potential of the constructivist power of collaborative small groups, and video-based peer discussion can be helpful in encouraging teachers to develop their own views and evidence-based interpretations. When peer observation is carried out for development, rather than for evaluative purposes, it provides the chance for teachers to work together, share ideas and knowledge, and discuss their problems and concerns.

Mercer et al. (2019) point to the particular value of video in creating a more dialogic and collaborative version of the relationship between theory and practice and allowing teachers to consider alternatives in a collaborative way. There is general agreement that it is valuable to collaboratively deconstruct and reconstruct practice in dialogue with another (Calandra et al., 2006). Borko et al. (2008) further suggest that providing a reflection framework and inviting teachers to choose their own reflection focus within a collaborative approach to reflection was preferred over reflecting individually on their videos. Borko et al. (2008, p. 417) share a viewpoint from a student teacher of just such a preference for collaboration:

> I think this [watching and discussing video clips] was the single most valuable part of the STAAR program. I have learned the most about my teaching by watching my teaching practice. Even better, though, was watching others teach a lesson that I also taught. My ideas have been sparked by others in this group. Having a safe place to watch ourselves and not feel like we were being criticized or evaluated was critical also.

Table 6.1. Benefits and caveats to peer observation (with and without video)

Benefits of both site-based and video-based peer observation	• Breaks down classroom walls and allows teachers to see others' practice • Teachers feel supported to make changes • Reduces sense of isolation • Provides opportunities to highlight exemplary practice • Feels more developmental than a supervisory observation • Creates an opportunity to learn from, and give feedback to peers • Is a core component of creating a professional community and building collective efficacy • Encourages collaboration and sharing that directly impacts student experiences • Helps teachers continue to improve their practice in ways that better promote student learning • Connects individuals to larger institutional instructional practices
Additional opportunities afforded through video-based peer observation	• No limitations resulting from distance, time zone, or aligning schedules with other observers • Allows for multiple observers for one lesson, beyond what could be accommodated in the physical classroom • Avoids 'surprises' as videos can be previewed before sharing • Promotes focused observations as videos can be selected around particular viewing targets • Videos can be available for review anywhere, anytime • Can be used to train teachers in specific instructional practices • Can be used to calibrate teachers in lesson appraisal • Can be used to role play feedback conversations
Cautions for both site-based and video-based peer observation	• Designate a facilitator for the peer-observation cycle • Ensure that observed teachers have voluntarily opted into the process • Develop observation skills prior to observing colleagues, focused on description rather than evaluation • Assign specific targets and ways to capture data during the observation • Use agreed protocols to support effective professional conversations during feedback sessions • Utilize artefacts such as lesson plans, curricular materials, and student work samples in conjunction with observation data
Additional cautions for video-based peer observation	• Consider the availability and usability of technology for recording • Determine staff expertise in using technology to support set-up and implementation • Address issues of privacy and consent from pupils and video-recorded teachers • Ensure videos are stored and accessed securely and are voluntarily provided by teachers, who should always retain ownership of the video

Kurtoglu-Hooton (2010) states that non-judgemental conditions are essential in peer-observation practice, and for these conditions to be realized, teachers must feel free to express their ideas and beliefs about teaching and learning, and mutual trust and respect between peers is crucial (Gosling, 2002). Borko et al. (2008) argue that this kind of safe space allows for constructive critique and the consideration of alternative pedagogical strategies. There is convincing evidence that video analysis of one's own teaching in groups needs careful handling, and that efforts to build empathy and trust in the group before this potentially face-threatening activity should be started to ensure a less face-threatening process:

> What we found was that for the VAS (Video Analysis Sessions) to be an effective space for both reflection and learner development, the participants must have a pre-established sense of rapport and feel that they are working within a comfort zone. Had the students not felt a sense of rapport, camaraderie, and positive emotions linked to their own teaching practices, the VAS might not have resulted in enhanced reflection. (Falter & Barnes, 2020, p. 18)

Just as reflection among novice teachers can be supported by a peer group discussion (Rich & Hannafin, 2009), the same principles can be applied to teacher educators collaborating with student teachers. Verlaan and Verlaan (2015, p. 155) offer a vision of what might be gained by teacher educators adopting a more collaborative approach:

> With guidance rather than instruction as their purpose, teacher educators would also take on a more collaborative than evaluative role, freeing up the intern to focus more on analysis and revision of practice than simply the evaluation of performance, and freeing up the educator to offer additional alternatives to the intern's thinking without the risk of suggesting to the intern that she or he is performing below standard. Cultivating a deliberate and methodical habit of reflection, and being empowered to select the standards of reflective practice and procedures to achieve them, an intern's choice to reflect will become a natural response to classroom experience.

One way to approach peer video-based learning design is as a 'critical friendship' (Smith, 2019). Critical friendship involves two or more teachers who have a peer relationship and can exchange and interact in order to reflect and articulate new understandings of practice (Farrell, 2008). Involving another colleague can help a teacher see classroom interaction and instruction through a student's perspective of the classroom (Estapa et al., 2016). Peers can collaboratively watch classroom events, and this works well within 'a video-mediated critical friendship reflection framework' (Smith, 2019, p.7). If such a process is structured and repeated, it has the capacity to help teachers make informed decisions about the subsequent teaching actions that are needed to improve teaching. The following vignette discusses such a trajectory.

Vignette: Video as a Key Element in an Innovative Peer-Observation Programme
Jaume Batlle
University of Barcelona

Peer observation is considered to be one of the most valued ways to promote professional development in the classroom (Gosling, 2002). Under this premise, many schools and education centres have established the use of peer-observation procedures to establish training programmes for their in-service teachers. In recent years, a number of ICT tools incorporating the use of video have been developed with the aim of helping teachers and other education stakeholders to develop observation practices. One example of such tools is Video Enhanced Observation (VEO) (Seedhouse, 2021). This app, which establishes video as a primary tool, was used to carry out the peer-observation programme that we present in this vignette.

This programme, created and reiterated twice by Education First Barcelona and the University of Barcelona, took place during the spring semesters of 2017 and 2018 (Batlle & Miller, 2017) and involved eight in-service Spanish as a Foreign Language teachers as participants in the project. Working together in groups of four pairs, all of the teachers were asked to observe two lessons delivered by their designated partner. The programme was developed as follows: firstly, all the teachers had a meeting to establish the aims of the observation and the corresponding grouping. Then, once the pairs were formed, each teacher observed their partner two times. Finally, after each lesson, both observer and teacher held a feedback meeting to talk about what had happened during the lessons regarding the specific professional development aims proposed in the project.

Throughout the peer-observation programme, the use of video took on particular special relevance, as it was used to record the lessons in order to carry out the feedback sessions. Every lesson was recorded through the use of VEO. The VEO system allows teachers to upload and easily share the video file via the online platform, along with notes and information from a tag system developed specifically for classroom observation. Consequently, the teacher was able to see the video before the feedback session, as all of the recordings were made available to all the participants of the peer-observation programme. Moreover, the teacher being observed was also able to read the observer's notes and comments, as all recorded information was uploaded as a whole. During the feedback sessions, teachers also used the video-recording information to develop their arguments. As a result, for both the observer and the teacher, video allowed them to easily focus their attention on specific points that they wanted to raise and address.

All of the teachers found the use of video very helpful for the peer-observation programme (Batlle & Miller, 2017), specifically during the feedback sessions (Batlle & Seedhouse, 2021), because they could use the video to sustain their comments and arguments with precise viewing of what had happened during the lessons. Thanks to the features of the VEO system, it was easier for teachers to find the specific moments upon which the feedback had been focused. Consequently, video and the use of VEO became helpful resources for teachers to develop a more data-led reflective practice within the peer-observation project.

In Batlle's vignette, it can be noticed that having a well-structured peer-observation learning design via video is highly beneficial for teachers as it facilitates co-constructed knowledge and reflection. At the same time, it can be assumed that, by repeating the model a few times, the peer relationship will be strengthened.

After teachers become comfortable with observing teaching on video – their own and others – and see the value in video as a rich material for learning about practice, they will benefit from interchange with trusted colleagues. It does not need to necessarily be formal; Whyte and Schmid (2018) have offered suggestions and supports for peers to use their phones and devices to informally capture peer video. As part of the ViLTE project she provided this resource on peer filming in teacher education: https://vilte.warwick.ac.uk/items/show/22. In addition, peer interchange does not need to begin with teachers sharing their own teaching but can start instead with a facilitator bringing in any video of teaching in order for the group to build a 'shared professional vision of teaching'. Sherin and van Es (2009) use the term 'shared professional vision' in reference to their work with mathematics teachers in 'video clubs': 'professional vision involves the ability to notice and interpret significant features of classroom interactions' (p. 22). The commonalities in what a group of teachers notice and how they interpret what they notice reinforces their mutual understandings of instructional practice.

'Video clubs' consist of a group of teachers who meet to view and discuss video excerpts, which are usually from each other's classrooms but may also be from other sources. A number of studies have provided accounts of video clubs, mostly in the USA, Europe, and Australia. Moore (2015) provides a detailed account of pre-service teachers in a video club setting and video clubs undoubtedly can provide the basis for collaborative teacher development (Sherin & Han, 2004). Within a video club, teachers make a commitment to meet, view, and discuss video recordings from participating teachers' classrooms, and examples of the kind of learning communities that can be established within such video clubs, as well as the kinds of teaching and learning conversations that result, have been well documented (Sherin & van Es, 2009).

Crichton et al. (2019), working with in-service teachers, suggests that even initial attempts to work collaboratively with video can encourage reflection, questioning, and interpreting significant features of practice and that this can be a good way to reinforce ongoing teacher learning. Teacher Activity Groups (TAGs) might also use video in a range of teacher development resources (see this example in Tejas, India https://www.youtube.com/watch?v=ao4AikxaIeo where a short British Council video introduces the concept of TAGs and outlines the structure for TAG meetings). Borg et al. (2020) provide a number of examples of the way video can be integrated into TAG teacher development activities.

Teacher educators can also be brought together as a peer group of their own to foster greater shared vision as faculty. In Baecher and Kung (2014), five teacher education faculty independently reviewed a video of student teacher practice, and then came together to collaboratively discuss it in a focus group. They were surprised to see what different lenses and perspectives each brought to the viewing and could see the implications the lack of shared vision might have in fostering a strong programme-level message about practice. For instance, in the field of TESOL, professional vision may be constructed and reinforced around approaches like Communicative Language Teaching, Content and Language Integrated Instruction, be readily identifiable through classic methods like Total Physical Response or the Language Experience Approach, or via lenses on practice like Teacher Talking Time (TTT) or Feedback on Form (recast versus elicitation). These approaches, methods, and theoretical considerations are our lingua franca and bind us together as a community of practice. However, we can easily make a lot of assumptions about what those really look like in action, especially when we only talk about them based on texts or in the abstract, rather than talking about them while also simultaneously viewing them.

Reflective Break

1. Teachers can work with video to reflect on their practice on an individual basis but also on a collaborative basis. Reflect on your experience of working

individually and with others. What are the possible benefits of these different ways of working?

2. Why is scaffolding of video viewing desirable? What are the most important ways to scaffold teachers through this process?

3. If you were to implement video club models in your institution, what criteria would you follow? Consider the choice of the facilitator, how often the meetings will take place, the length of each meeting, who would be invited and the focus of the discussion.

4. Read this excerpt from Luna & Sherin (2017) from a video club model meeting.

(The discussion was taking place while they were watching the video of a science lesson.)

Carol: He is moving up and down.

Rachel: It's like a [grunts and shrugs her body down].

Facilitator: So he's saying when the alcohol is cold or when [the water is] cold the alcohol is cold or something, so he's scrunching down. And then he says 'it tries to get up'. So what is he doing there? What is he trying to say by that?

Rachel: I don't know, was he…hmmm? But I think that he was using his body to explain what was happening. See, because I understood that the idea was, when it's cold I do this [shrugs down], you know when it's hot, I do that [sits up tall]. So they relate the alcohol by maybe that way.

Facilitator: So what you're saying is maybe they are saying alcohol behaves in a way that they would behave if they were cold or hot?

Rachel: Because that's the prior knowledge that they have. They don't know anything about liquids, but they're relating cold and hot…

Carol: It expands out.

Rachel: He says escape. 'Maybe the alcohol, it's trying to escape from the cold water and the hot water.'

Facilitator: So what do you think he understands here?

Carol: I think he understands that liquids react to hot and cold temperatures. Oh, and I think he knows that for something to move it needs energy. But I don't think he connects his ideas or understands that heat is the energy that causes the red substance to move. Not yet.

Rachel: You know, for him, that's a good explanation. I mean with all of the prior knowledge they know, they only know about the alcohol moving up and down, that's all they know. But Leo uses his experiences with hot and cold temperatures to try to explain what he is seeing. And actually the way a thermometer works is when you do put it in that hot water, and the

> *liquid rises up, it's doing that in reaction to the hot water, so his explanation makes sense, right? Even if he's not using the word 'expanding'. He has the idea that is what the liquid is doing.*
>
> - How did teachers and facilitator co-construct meaning?
> - How effective were the facilitator's questions? Would you have asked different questions to the teachers?
> - Did teachers mainly describe, evaluate, or interpret students' behaviours and ideas?

STRUCTURED APPROACHES TO PEER OBSERVATION WITH VIDEO

Video can offer groups of teachers a chance to examine particular pedagogical practices common to the ELT world, specific practices tied to a local approach or curriculum, or provide the opportunity for shared viewing of particular student challenges at a site. However, the video material is only as effective in group professional learning as the facilitation. The facilitator of a peer viewing group could be a teacher leader, a coach, consultant, or a supervisor. No matter who is facilitating, the facilitation process itself appears to be essential for the success of peer observation.

If a shared professional vision is the desired outcome, time for teachers to learn descriptive observation techniques, for careful observation, and for reflective discussion that can allow for criticality and honesty need to be provided. Thus, the construction of a shared professional vision among a group of teachers depends not only on the use of video as a material, but also a clear protocol for facilitation. In their review of dozens of research articles on video analysis, Baecher et al. (2018b) found that there is a lack of specificity about such facilitation processes. The process could involve regular video-based discussions, use of a structured viewing guide with open-ended questions, a checklist with closed-ended items to look for, or a note-taking form to shape the data collection process. Here, we offer several possible approaches that have been used successfully to facilitate peer observation of teaching using video.

Sample Peer-Observation Approach: Using Group Structures

The context and purpose for peer observation are also important factors in the decision to use video. Various approaches may be good fits depending on the nature and goals of the peer-observation scheme. The Australian Institute for Teaching and School Leadership (https://www.aitsl.edu.au/lead-develop/develop-others/ classroom-observation/classroom-observation-strategies) has a number of videos and supporting materials along with suggested variations on peer observation that are highly structured and utilize group formats, including: *instructional rounds*, *learning walks*, and *lesson study*. In all three approaches, video can be swapped in for live, on-site observation, as outlined in Table 6.2.

Table 6.2. Types of structured peer observation

Peer-observation approach	Phases (adapted from AITSL)		Video opportunities
Instructional rounds	1.	School leadership identifies a 'problem of practice' as the focus for the observations.	Instead of a group of teachers physically going to several classrooms, video records from classrooms can be posted and 'virtual' Instructional Rounds can take place in one facilitated session. Discussion of data observed can also be carried out virtually.
	2.	Observation groups of 3–5 teachers collect data related to the identified 'problem of practice'.	
	3.	Observer group visits a range of classrooms to locate evidence (15–20 minutes per classroom).	
	4.	Observers make detailed, non-judgemental notes.	
	5.	Groups debrief after observations using agreed protocols.	
	6.	Groups identify patterns, wonderings, recommendations across the school related to the 'problem of practice'.	
	7.	Groups build a picture of teaching and learning throughout the school, not just of individual classrooms.	
	8.	Groups make recommendations for next stage of work.	
Learning walks	1.	Teachers have pre-walk meeting with facilitator and group to establish and clarify focus of the walk.	Participating teachers can share video from their lessons around a central focus. Peers can view each other's video and then each teacher can have the chance to debrief with colleagues. All of the steps can take place in an online platform as well.
	2.	Observation in groups of 2–4 teachers (approximately 10 minutes per classroom).	
	3.	Discreet interaction with observed teacher and/or students may occur if appropriate.	
	4.	Short debrief immediately following observation (often outside the classroom visited).	
	5.	Group engages in reflective conversation, sharing observations (detailed, non-judgemental).	
	6.	Group repeats observations and debrief conversations in successive classrooms until scheduled visits completed.	
	7.	Group shares findings formally or informally, as agreed, to the participants and the whole school.	

(*Continued*)

Table 6.2 (*Continued*)

Peer-observation approach	Phases (adapted from AITSL)	Video opportunities
Lesson study	1. A pair or small group of teachers who teach the same course co-plan a lesson, with a focus on a shared pedagogical challenge. 2. In the first classroom observation, the plan is used by one teacher to teach the lesson and group members observe the lesson and take notes, with a focus on what the students are doing and understanding. 3. The group meets for a post-observation discussion and the lesson plan is revised and amended based on the group discussion. 4. In the second classroom observation a different group member teaches the revised lesson plan with a different class and group members observe and take notes. 5. In the final discussion, the group meets again to discuss both observed lessons, make final adjustments to the lesson plan, and share results school-wide.	Rather than having to go observe the shared lesson, which may conflict with other teachers' schedules, the lesson can be video recorded, and the group can all access it later that day. The follow-up conversation and revised lesson can also be held via online video chat.

Sample Peer-Observation Approach: One-to-One Virtual Visits

There are many available resources to support the implementation of one-to-one classroom intervisitation, enabling individual teachers to get the benefits of peer observation without a structured group format. This one-to-one approach also requires a process and protocols but can be left to pairs of teachers to negotiate among themselves and essentially self-facilitate. Most resources for peer observation do recommend a pre/while/post set-up, so that both the observer and the observed have clear and shared expectations for the experience and the feedback session. Usually, this involves a type of written communication or contract around the peer observation.

The introduction of video, apart from the usual demands of the technology, logistics, and sharing of the video, can make the one-to-one peer observation relatively simple to carry out. Table 6.3 presents a sample pre/while/post template from Victoria Education and Training (https://www.education.vic.gov.au/school/teachers/teachingresources/practice/improve/Pages/peerobservation.aspx), adapted for use with video and for an ELT classroom context.

Table 6.3. Planning the peer observation: template for video-based observation/ELT

Discussion of the peer-observation process

Background and goals

Consideration of outcomes, concerns, or hesitations for the peer observation and implications for the planned peer observation. Selection of goals of and focus for the observation*.

What are the learning goals for the observing teacher? For the observed teacher?

Observation data

How the observer will observe, collect, interpret, and store their observation data, using the observation template.

What types of evidence will the observing teacher gather? What protocol will be used? How will the evidence be recorded?

Logistics

Confirmation of the class, date, and time for the observation to occur, and the video to be shared, including a timely post-observation conversation.

Which class will be recorded, and what will the focus be for that lesson? How and when will the observer access the recording? What communication channels will be used prior to the observation?

Impact

The conduit and process for enabling the learning to inform whole-school practices (for example professional learning communities, whole-school instructional practice, curriculum planning).

In what way will the observation relate to school-wide goals? How will the learning be shared beyond the peer observation?

**10 Focus Area Possibilities Common to ELT Observation*

1. Teacher Talking Time (TTT) versus Student Talking Time
2. Nominations (using student names/calling on students to respond/wait time)
3. Tasks (clarity/variation/open-closed/movement/pacing/monitoring groupwork)
4. Interaction patterns (T-whole class/T-student/S-S/S)
5. Materials (content/intelligibility/quality/coherence/amount)
6. Linguistic areas (meaning/form-grammar/pronunciation/lexical/functions)
7. Errors (anticipation of predicted errors/response to errors)
8. Instructions (use of board/checking for understanding/modelling)
9. Inductive approach (elicitation/language analysis)
10. Use of board (clarity/utility)

During and post the peer observation

(a) Sight observation(s)

What did you see the teacher and the students doing in relation to the agreed focus area*?

(b) Sound observation(s)

What did you hear the teacher and students saying in relation to the agreed focus area?

(c) Evidence

Tailor this space to record specific measures according to the agreement during the pre-observation conversation and directly related to the observation focus.

(Continued)

Table 6.3 (*Continued*)

During and post the peer observation

(d) Celebrations

What aspects of the observation went well?

What aspects of the observation should be shared with relevant collegiate groups?

(e) Questions

The observer might have questions to clarify with the teacher after the observations or thoughts which can be listed here.

(f) Opportunities

Was there anything that might be done differently to enhance student learning?

> **Reflective Break**
> 1. How was your last peer-observation experience? How positive or negative was it?
> 2. What recommendations would you offer to a teacher who is new to peer observation?
> 3. How important is a pre-observation meeting for you? What could teachers talk about then?

INTEGRATING PEER AND SELF-OBSERVATION WITH VIDEO

As we have seen, once a procedure is in place, there are many rewards to seeing other teachers teach. Peer observation, when implemented thoughtfully, is beneficial to teacher learning and can foster a school-wide view of observation and feedback as developmental (DuFour & Eaker, 1998), while working towards a shared professional vision.

In the excerpt below from a study on the use of video in an induction training program for new EFL teachers to examine their Teacher Talking Time (TTT) (Mercado & Baecher, 2014), the elements described in this and previous chapters come together within an institutional initiative. Focused observation, the use of video, teacher self-observation, and the application of micro-ethnographic viewing techniques all combined in this case to reduce overall TTT across dozens of classrooms.

Institutional Initiative using Video-Based Self-Observation

Founded in 1938, the Instituto Cultural Peruano Norteamericano (ICPNA) is a binational centre that promotes the cultural exchange between Peru and the United

States, by teaching the English and Spanish languages. At ICPNA, self-observation through video has not only helped hundreds of EFL teachers grow professionally on their own, it has also served a higher purpose at the program and institutional level by contributing directly to organizational change. One example is the 2007 'Teacher Talk Time' (TTT) Reduction Campaign. In this professional development initiative, self-observation through video provided teachers and administrators with an ideal means to gauge results progressively and make adjustments in regard to the measures being taken to support these projects.

The decision to initiate a campaign to reduce TTT in ICPNA's classrooms came as a result of an extensive evaluation of the academic study program, faculty, and other aspects that could influence the teaching and learning process at the Institute. There was a need to increase *student talk time* (STT) significantly and reduce excessive, non-productive *teacher talk time* (TTT) as much as possible. The project proceeded through the following stages:

1. Development of the campaign and setting of a timeline for implementation.
2. Development of instruments, protocols, performance metrics, support systems, and criteria for outcomes.
3. Introduction of the campaign to teachers, and collection of their input on the process; training on STT versus excessive TTT, TTT reduction strategies, self-assessment techniques through self-observation; development of goal statements and action plans on the part of the teachers.
4. Self-observations done by teachers at all of the branches. Formative post-observation discussion sessions with mentor supervisors and action plan adjustments.
5. First assessment of outcomes and follow-up action plans.
6. Final round of self-observations and assessments.
7. Culmination of campaign. Follow-up teacher-training and professional development initiatives.

In step 3, for example, the campaign was launched with an in-service teacher development (TD) session that presented the rationale for the campaign and the action plan to be followed by each of the stakeholders, most particularly the teachers. The session was presented as follows:

- *Introduction:* What are TTT and STT? Why is STT good for the program? How is the difference productive and what is excessive TTT?
- *Demo videos:* Demonstration of two classes: one showing excessive TTT and another one that prioritizes STT.
- *General campaign strategy:* Presentation of the TTT Reduction campaign strategy and timeline.

- *Self-assessment stage:* Description of strategies, protocols, instruments, and desired outcomes. Practice using the STT-TTT self-assessment checklist.
- *Comprehension check activities:* Activities to make certain that teachers understand the overall message and their role in the process.

The TD session was crucial in getting the program off to an auspicious beginning. Teachers were able to understand why the campaign was being initiated, their roles in the process, how they could self-assess to make certain they were making progress, and what the desired outcomes were. At the same time, they were informed as to how they were expected to work collaboratively with their mentor supervisors in order to maximize their chances of reaching the ultimate goal. Table 6.4 displays

Table 6.4. Targeted self-assessment tool for video review

#	Behaviours conducive to increasing STT	Observed	Behaviours conducive to increasing TTT	Observed
1.	The teacher's explanations are concise and opportune.		The teacher gives long and unnecessary instructions or explanations.	
2.	The teacher elicits from students when presenting new language.		The teacher does not elicit from students enough when presenting new language.	
3.	The teacher encourages students to ask questions.		The teacher asks questions when there is an opportunity for students to do so.	
4.	The teacher offers students opportunities to summarize and/or paraphrase.		The teacher summarizes and/or paraphrases when there is an opportunity for students to do so.	
5.	The teacher only expresses opinions and facts that are relevant to the lesson.		The teacher gives opinions about facts and ideas that are not relevant to the lesson.	
6.	The teacher encourages students to add information to their classmates' responses.		The teacher adds additional information to students' responses when it is not conducive to more STT.	
7.	The teacher encourages students to answer her/his questions as well as their classmates'.		The teacher poses questions and then answers them her/himself.	
8.	The teacher has students do the wrap-up.		The teacher does not involve students in the wrap-up.	
9.	The teacher provides students with enough wait time and prep/thinking time.		The teacher does not provide enough wait or prep/thinking time to students.	
10.	The teacher refrains from unnecessarily repeating what she/he or the students have said.		The teacher repeats unnecessarily what she/he or the students have said.	

the instrument that was provided to teachers and used as a self-assessment checklist for STT-TTT that could be utilized during video-playback.

In this case, video was an essential tool in promoting the self-appraisal that changed classroom practice, and supported student learning. Participant teachers commented:

> When you watch a video, you have a better chance to see what's really going on with your whole class, something you might not be able to do in the classroom. At a given moment in a video, you can tell, for example, what students are using English and what students are not. This is an area in which self-observation through video has helped me a lot.
>
> There are many ways it has helped me in many areas. I think something important is that by watching myself teach, I was able not only to experience being a student in my own class, but also to observe other students' reactions to my teaching. I think this has helped me to focus the activities more towards the students and to consider their needs and learning styles.

When essential elements of video review in peer and self-observation are present and highly scaffolded and facilitated, the results can be powerful and widespread.

Reflective Break

1. What are the advantages of doing peer observation with video rather than in-person in your school or institution?
2. Watch this video clip: https://www.youtube.com/watch?v=c_W6tb35r3M.
   - How could the peer-observation stages (pre-observation meeting, observation, post-observation meeting) be adapted to video?
   - Do you believe the observer's noticing remarks would be the same if she was observing an online lesson? Why or why not?
   - How might the peer-observation process be combined with self-observation?

Chapter 7

Role of Video in Supervision

INTRODUCTION

For many educators, the first use of video with teachers that springs to mind is its use in evaluation or observer feedback sessions. However, Chapters 4, 5, and 6 provide a strong rationale, as well as a variety of concrete approaches, for beginning the process of video analysis in a descriptive, non-evaluative manner and beginning with looking at teaching generally, then moving to viewing oneself and viewing one's own and the practice of peers before engaging in review for a clearly evaluative purpose. This evaluative feedback may come from a supervisor in the workplace, in pre-service teacher education, or from a coach or mentor. Although we use the term 'supervisor', much of what is contained in this chapter is relevant for mentors or coaches who are asked to engage with teachers in order to improve and assess their practice. We purposely situate the topic of how video can be used in supervision and by supervisors *after* the earlier chapters in this text, thus emphasizing that the best results come from teachers first experiencing video in numerous low-stakes, intriguing, and positive ways prior to engaging with it in high-stakes assessment contexts. So much of supervision could be developmental and teacher-led, but the reality is that most teachers experience a sense of anxiety when it comes time to be formally observed by a supervisor because it is evaluative and supervisor-led.

In this chapter, we explore how the introduction of video into the supervisory process can be made less stressful – rather than more so – when video is introduced. Video review can enable teachers to become self-assessors as part of the supervision cycle, and supervisors can also be invited to engage in self-review of their conferencing skills. We focus on three ways video supports teacher learning in supervisory contexts: the affordances of video in combination with on-site observation, the long-term benefits to teachers of a program of video-based supervision, and a video enhanced analysis tool (VEO, www.veo.co.uk). We also take an in-depth look at how video supports supervisor learning, an area we believe receives too little attention given the pivotal role of supervisors in teacher evaluation and growth. Whether for teachers or for supervisors, we contend that video can serve as a disruptive ingredient when introduced into the usual approaches and it can be used to shape supervision into a more learning-oriented professional development experience.

COMBINING VIDEO WITH ON-SITE SUPERVISION

As discussed in Chapter 6, video self- and peer observation can be truly enlightening, especially when a narrow focus is applied and the emphasis is placed on noticing and reflecting on small moments of practice, rather than evaluating and rating overall performance. However, at times there is a need for a more formal evaluation of teaching. When formal evaluation is needed, video can serve to foster teacher voice in that process. At first, it might seem that video in conjunction with supervision would add to teachers' stress – but if teachers have learned to look descriptively, see the value of video review in learning more about their own practice, and have become comfortable sharing their video with peers – video can upend the traditional power dynamic present in traditional observation while still fulfilling the evaluative requirements of the process.

Traditionally, academic supervisors are viewed by teachers with a certain mistrust because their role is primarily evaluative or judgemental in nature, with consequences that involve hiring, promotion, and salary decisions. The supervisor is positioned as 'expert' and is likely to control the agenda of the meeting and dominate the discussion with the observee (Webb, 2020), who, on the other hand, usually plays a more passive role. Thus, the inherent view of supervisors as assessors has direct implications for the kinds of interactions that take place in the observation and feedback cycle. This plays out in a few ways. One result of highly evaluative, directive supervision is that teachers associate the supervisory observation cycle (pre-meeting, lesson observation, post-observation conference) as a ritualistic, artificial exercise, with teachers 'depicting...supervision as a negative experience and supervisors as bureaucratic administrators' (Kayaoglu, 2012).

Another concern is that supervisors may lack experience in ELT, or if trained in ELT, lack training in supervision (Körkkö, 2019). Supervisors may treat every teacher as 'equal', going through the same processes in a uniform way with all teachers. When supervision approaches are applied in a monolithic manner, they may not always be a good fit with the diversity of teachers, their concerns, their levels of background experience, or their teaching styles (Pajak, 2003). Additionally, supervisors may be more focused on completing the evaluation process than tuned in to where the teacher is in terms of particular areas for growth and development. Just as we discuss the need for differentiation in instruction, supervision too warrants differentiated approaches. Finally, even with the best of intentions, research has repeatedly shown that in these conversations, supervisors tend to tell rather than listen, prescribe rather than probe, and evaluate rather than empower (Farr, 2010). Post-observation supervisory talk is generally controlled by supervisors because it is they who reconstruct the observed lesson based on their notes and memory of events.

In order to lay the foundation for a supportive and non-judgemental relationship between teacher and supervisor that differs from other less productive, strictly evaluative scenarios, teachers must believe that the main goal of the academic supervisor sitting in front of them is not simply to complete a necessary requirement, but rather, that the supervisor is truly interested in and invested in the teacher's learning and professional growth (Chamberlin, 2000). When teachers experience supervisory interactions as clearly teacher-centred, the very nature of their relationship is likely to change and so is the teacher's authentic engagement. Introducing self-observation through video into the supervision cycle can support the development of a more horizontal relationship between teacher and supervisor; when handled thoughtfully, video review can dramatically shift the nature of the post-observation conference talk and the relationship teachers have with the supervision process.

A concrete way to make the observation cycle more teacher-centred is to invite teachers and supervisors to video record the lesson, thus affording teachers the opportunity to analyse their own performance. When the supervisor and the candidate have reviewed the lesson on video, *both* parties enter the POC (Post-observation conference) with observation data to discuss. Teachers' video review of their taught lesson has been shown to vastly increase teacher talk in the post-observation conference, with teachers describing, noticing, suggesting, and holding the floor to a much greater extent than when they have not viewed their lesson via video (Baecher & McCormack, 2012, 2015). This suggests that adding video review to traditional observation practices has the potential to disrupt typical supervisor-dominated patterns of feedback.

Table 7.1 outlines some of the ways that video-based observation differs from on-site observation, and this can be used to consider where they can be used in conjunction with each other. We are not advising the elimination of on-site observation – we are suggesting, however, that adding on video review to traditional observation brings in a number of powerful affordances.

Table 7.1. Features of on-site and video-based observation for teacher evaluation

Traditional in-person observation in teacher evaluation	Video-based observation in teacher evaluation
Supervisor captures observational data.	The camera captures observational data.
Calibration of scoring for the observed lesson cannot take place unless multiple viewers visit the same class at the same time.	Calibration of scoring for the observed lesson can take place as multiple viewers can assess the same lesson simultaneously or over a period of time.
The observer is the one with the authority, memory, and data to assess the lesson.	The observed teacher and the observer can both assess the lesson.
During the post-observation conference, where teacher and observer have perceptual differences the observer's notes are used.	During the post-observation conference, the video can be consulted when teacher and observer have perceptual differences.

Reflective Break

1. What are your experiences with supervision? What do you remember as a particularly negative supervisory experience? What about one that you found truly supportive?
2. Have you ever been supervised using video of your teaching? Did it change the nature of the post-observation in this case?
3. Have you ever supervised a teacher using video of their teaching? How did you employ the video as part of your observation and feedback cycle?
4. To what extent is it more productive to follow a framework for supervisory POC?

THE USE OF VIDEO FOR DISTANCE SUPERVISION

In contexts where video-based supervision is exclusively the means through which supervision takes place, for example in distance supervision or distance teaching, the affordances outlined in Table 7.1 are useful to consider. Too often, even with a video record of the teaching readily available – as they are when using videoconferencing platforms for the lesson's delivery – supervision still takes place as if the teacher had never seen their lesson. For instance, a lesson might be video-recorded as it was delivered remotely through Zoom, then the video is shared with the supervisor. At the post-observation conference, the supervisor and teacher review the video – also via Zoom – but the supervisor proceeds to review what took place, make observations, and dominate the talk. Therefore, the potential for the video to enhance the quality of the supervisory interaction is truncated, because the teacher is not explicitly asked to review their own teaching and come to the conference prepared to participate as a collaborator.

In fact, one of the most useful aspects of video in supervision is the possibility it generates for remote supervision. When teachers are geographically distant or spread out across a large urban area, supervision can occur with video being shared through online platforms. The same is true for providing supervision when the instruction is remote, or when the supervisor lives at a distance from the school site or needs to visit multiple teachers in a single day. In all of these instances, it is helpful to have a very structured protocol to guide the teacher through self-observation prior to meeting for an online video conference to discuss the lesson. Doing so creates more clarity around the expectations for the conversation. Depending on the local priorities, current teaching initiatives, evaluation standards, or past performance, a set of steps can be designed to guide the process. Table 7.2 provides a sample set of protocol questions that could be provided to teachers prior to discussing their lesson with their supervisor.

Table 7.2. Video-based supervision: guiding questions for teachers

The following questions should be completed after you have reviewed your teaching, and before sharing the video with your supervisor.	
How was the design of this lesson uniquely tailored to your group of learners?	In answering this question, be sure to consider your students' experiences, strengths, and learning needs. Even if this lesson fits into a mandated curriculum, you must explain how it was designed for your particular class – referencing their funds of knowledge and informal and/or formal assessment[s].
What target language did you plan for *and then see students using* in this lesson? Please provide a timestamp of 3–5 minutes from your video that captures evidence (or lack) of students' target language (grammar/vocabulary/pronunciation, etc.).	What was the language objective, and what did you notice in your enactment of the language objective? Did students meet the language objective? Where do you see evidence of this?
Reflect on the observation process. What did you learn in this lesson/supervision/feedback cycle about your students and/or about yourself?	What was surprising to you? What did you see that appeared contrary to your expectations/planning/philosophies? What was challenging as you reviewed your video?
What are *one or two* actions you will take between now and your next observation to better support student development of English language proficiency?	For each action, please explain why you chose it, and what resources (human or otherwise) you will draw upon to help you meet it.

Vignette: Supervision via Video in Distance Practicum
John Hughes
ELT writer, Teacher Trainer and Materials Writer

I use video more and more because using your phone is so easy. I don't show the whole class back to a trainee but pick out relevant sections to focus on. If the teacher wants to watch the whole lesson back, they can in their own time. I also tend to choose a focus for the observation and video sometimes helps and sometimes it doesn't. For example, looking at a teacher's gestures is obviously helped with video. You can turn the sound off and see if you more or less understand instructions from the gestures or record what the teacher says and analyse how clear the language is. In a survey, I ran lots of teachers an extra perspective and as an observer in teacher feedback, the video supports your message. Sometimes showing the video is more effective than giving verbal feedback because the teacher can see what is happening and what to work on just by watching (not you telling).

When teachers are well-prepared to enter into the post-observation conference, they can do more of the noticing, describing, analysing, and making recommendations for future practice. In this way, video creates a space for teachers to become their own supervisors – they need not rely on memories of the lesson, or the supervisors' notes and impressions to guide their reflection. However, supervisors must also be willing to downshift from their role expectations. Instead of being the ones to notice, point out, describe, analyse, and make recommendations, they can become facilitators of those processes. By doing so, supervisors can also better assess what teachers already know and are able to do, and avoid bringing in terminology, ideas, and suggestions that are not going to be taken up by teachers (Golombek, 2011). The power dynamic is reshaped through the introduction of the video and the delayed feedback timeline, which allows teachers to self-appraise before meeting with supervisors. In the next section, we explore how video can assist supervisors in making these shifts so that they can better serve as facilitators of teacher growth.

Reflective Break
1. We read about many benefits of video in supervision when teaching is at a distance from the supervisor, or during remote instruction. What are some of the limitations? How could those be addressed?
2. What do you believe would support teachers doing more of the self-appraisal work with video, or other artefacts of teaching, prior to conversations with supervisors? What would supervisors need to give up to achieve these goals?

> 3. As a teacher, if you were given the option to choose of being observed in a face-to-face lesson, synchronously in an online lesson (the supervisor joins your lesson at the scheduled time) or asynchronously via a recorded video lesson, which option would you prefer and why?

CONNECTING LESSON PLANNING TO INSTRUCTION THROUGH VIDEO SUPERVISION

In some observation and feedback cycles, supervisors discuss teachers' lesson plans, then observe instruction, and then meet to debrief the lesson. When a lesson plan conference can be held before the observation takes place, these pre-observation meetings can be very supportive of teacher learning and go far to enlighten supervisors, for as they hear teachers' reasoning about their planning it gives insight into the teacher's knowledge and skills, and what is likely to be important to look at during the observation. It can also be a step towards a more collaborative relationship, as the supervisor and teacher both become vested in the success of the lesson. Pre-observation lesson conversations lend themselves to a 'I'm here to help you plan a successful lesson' rather than a 'I'm here to catch you being unsuccessful' orientation. When both supervisor and teacher know they will be video recording the lesson to subsequently examine certain features, this very knowledge tends to contribute to lessons in which teachers definitively attempt to enact the practice.

Once the lesson has taken place and been video-recorded (either with or without the supervisor present), the post-observation conference should take place only after the teacher has had the opportunity to first independently review the video. Depending on the focus that was set during the pre-observation conference, the post-observation review can identify those moments during the video-recorded lesson where there is evidence of that practice to explore. If there was no pre-observation conference, a review of the video can still offer rich data about the instruction in relation to what the teacher had originally planned or intended. For instance, Kaneko-Marques (2015), working in a teacher education context in Brazil, studied the impact of video on the focus of the post-observation conference talk and noted that both the teacher (partner teachers Henry and Fred in this excerpt) and supervisor were able to go to the beliefs that Henry and Fred had in mind during their planning, which they noticed in their video review were not realized.

> In one of these post-observation sessions, two future teachers, Henry and Fred, mentioned after watching their first class recordings that their classroom procedures were mainly ruled by grammar-translation

techniques and that their activities were teacher-centred. They were surprised to see that they were reproducing teaching models they did not believe in or support, as they realized that their pedagogical discourse diverged from their classroom practices. These future teachers concluded that having the opportunity to watch their classes and to reflect on their own practice helped them identify and solve pedagogical problems in their classrooms...

In the first classes taught by Henry and Fred, the proposed activities were teacher-centred, and students performed them individually. Vocabulary building was based on lists and translations, and grammar instruction was ruled by traditional perspectives because they conceived grammar structure as an object to be explicitly presented and decoded... It was interesting to notice that Henry and Fred perceived 'something wrong' in their lessons, as they commented that the lessons needed to be more dynamic. The proposed activity to place students in pairs or in groups would make their lessons more student-centred and would favour students' interaction.

In their next lessons, they implemented these changes, so the activities were performed in pairs and in groups and focused on reading and discussing a text using reading strategies. Students had to try to solve the comprehension questions on their own without using a dictionary. To correct the activity, the student teachers suggested that students check their classmates' answers, using peer correction instead of teacher correction. (pp. 72–73)

This exchange provides a sense of how the video can serve as an external measure of performance – unbiased, objective – that teachers (with supervisor facilitation) can use to adjust or alter their course of action. When teachers see that certain results are apparent in the video, they can then go to their plan and consider what changes to make to reach different results. While this exchange between Henry and Fred focuses on the very concrete aspects of how they would move to use more pairs and groups, it is in these concrete moves a world of teaching philosophies are revealed. Especially when examining a full supervisory cycle – from lesson plan to video of lesson delivery, deeper themes that underscore specific pedagogical moves may emerge, such as those in Figure 7.1.

Supervisors and teachers may find that the mental distance offered by video review – where the supervisor can focus more on what the teacher sees, and the teacher need not rely on memory alone to discuss practice – can offer a chance to go

Figure 7.1. Teaching philosophies that can be explored in full-lesson review

deeper than the usual recap of events that takes up much of supervisory conference time. As Crookes (2016, p.73) states:

> Language teaching is a value-laden enterprise and we would do well to recognize that. It should help, conceptually, for us to notice that both the language teaching practices we deliver, engage with, have been inculcated with, themselves have values or philosophies underlying them.

When there is no mental distance, and no physical artefacts to ground the conversation, supervisor conversations lead to a reliance on memory of events rather than analysis of evidence. When a video record has also been made of the lesson, combining these two objects: the lesson plan with the video – can elevate the nature of supervision and is especially positive for more experienced teachers. They can, effectively, analyse their own lessons with minimal facilitation from the supervisor. Engaging teachers and supervisors in this new way of 'doing' supervision based on data can be an effective and developmental change. The vignette below describes the interrelationship that develops between planning, video analysis, and reflection as a systematic approach to supervision that actually reduces supervisor workload and encourages teacher ownership of their reflection.

Vignette: Video of Practice to Support Lesson Planning and Reflection
Roger Saulsman (Principal, St. Helena's Primary School in Ellenbrook, Australia)

We identified videos of practice as being suitable for our school because of the need to accelerate the improvement and development of teachers. We were looking for tools that weren't human resource-intensive, and video was a really good way for us to achieve that, once teachers had an understanding of what it was that they were building their capacity towards.

We first sat down as a leadership team and looked at how other schools had used videos. Most of it was used around self-reflection. There are challenges in implementing videos of practice. Any change has challenges to it. Teachers are resistant and reluctant to take on new approaches, and so we had to do this gently. We had to make sure that we selected carefully the people that were initially approached to come on board with video in their practice. We went to, obviously, the more confident ones, and worked with them and asked them permission for 'Can we now share this work that we've done using video with other members of staff?'. And once we started to go down that line and teachers could see that this was a non-threatening, quite 'non-invasive' approach that was beneficial both to them and to their peers, they jumped on board.

After six, eight, ten months of videoing themselves and us using those videos at staff meetings or inductions processes, people started to see that it became a really valuable tool within their classroom, to a point where 90% of our staff were happy to use the video and self-reflect on them. Staff members will sit down with an administrator and we discuss their goals – what they want to achieve. And once we've decided together what we want to achieve, we'll then go in, we'll video their lesson, we'll provide some feedback. They'll do a self-reflection on their video, and then we'll come together and talk about how their lesson went and where they can improve.

From those meetings, we'll decide 'what would you like to work on next' or 'what could you do to make your lessons better'. And then, once we've decided on our following goal or action, then we'll go in and we'll use the video, or we'll do the observations again. And it's a cyclical process. We'll meet with them every few weeks depending on their expertise in teaching and also how new they are in the school. (https://www.aitsl.edu.au/tools-resources/resource/videos-of-practice)

Directors of schools can support the inclusion of video into the supervision approach with great success, as seen here and in Chapter 6 where the ICPNA program of using video in supervision reduced teacher talk through teacher self-assessment in combination with supervisor support. Using a tagging tool can make it easier for the supervisor and the observed teacher to go directly to key moments for discussion. One technological development that can be considered in tagging for the POC is the Video Enhanced Observation (VEO, www.veo.co.uk) application developed at Newcastle University, UK. We have previously mentioned this app in previous chapters. What follows provides more detail of the VEO process.

The VEO app was designed as a tool for reflection that can be used in various fields including education. It aims to create a network of good practices via video-tagging. The app enables the user to tag significant moments while recording a lesson or practice and once the recording and tagging is done the tag-sets can be viewed as statistics to get a general understanding of the lesson or they can be used to jump to specific parts of the recording.

The recorded videos can be uploaded to and stored on a web-based portal named VEO portal. The portal allows users to create personal profiles, professional communities, and networks. Users can review their videos, search for specific tags, and invite other users to watch and comment on their videos. The technology also provides the opportunity for users to upload different format videos directly to the portal without using the app on a mobile device (iPad) and tag retrospectively. It seems that issues raised on using video for reflection such as the challenge of learning to edit videos, finding appropriate equipment, software, and suitable storage facilities can be resolved by the use of VEO. There is a large Erasmus+ project, including six partners from five different countries, aiming to improve the quality of teaching and learning via the VEO app called VEO Europa (VEO Europa, 2017). Furthermore, there is the British Council ELTRA-funded research project that looked into reflection among teachers through the use of the SETT (Self-Evaluation of Teacher Talk) framework (Urmeneta & Walsh, 2017; Walsh, 2006, 2011, 2013) and the VEO app (Miller, 2015). Sert (2019) states that VEO provides opportunities for stimulated recall. Additionally, Çelik, Baran, and Sert's study (2018) concluded that the use of video-tagging mobile application creates affordances for data-led reflection and observation. This claim is also supported by Haines and Miller (2016 cited in Sert, 2019), who strongly believe that observations through video-tagging analysis get visually empowered.

Reflective Break

Examine this sample lesson plan and the video record of the teaching of this lesson. If you were the supervisor of this teacher, what questions might you have asked about their lesson plan? What questions would connect to what is visible in the video recording of the lesson?

https://www.youtube.com/watch?v=5Re-FWcA03I

Lesson plan outline

- Stage 1 – Teacher introduces the topic, shows a picture, and gives students time to talk about the picture. Students then talk in pairs.
- Stage 2 – Teachers asks students to share their ideas with the group.
- Stage 3 – Teacher asks students to read the text to spot 'past simple structures'. Students then share their answers with the group.

- Stage 4 – Teacher elicits target language from students and writes sentences on the whiteboard. She focuses on the form and meaning of the target language (teaching the simple past tense).
- Stage 5 – Teacher drills some sentences. Students repeat individually and as a group.
- Stage 6 – Teacher models intonation (stress). She also elicits target language from students regarding the pronunciation of -ed endings.
- Stage 7 – Controlled practice. Students practise saying sentences by changing them from simple present to simple past and filling in the blanks.
- Stage 8 – Students practise their sentences in pairs by asking and answering questions.

VIDEO USED FOR SUPERVISOR LEARNING

Most of the past few chapters have focused on how teachers can reflect on and learn about classroom practice via analysis of their own or others' videos. Often, this takes place as a part of the observation and feedback cycle guided by supervisors or coaches. Ironically, though, these same supervisors or coaches who facilitate teacher learning may not ever have the opportunity to examine *their* feedback practices using video. In this section, we examine how supervisors may use video for self-reflection.

The work of supervision is greatly undervalued – most supervisors are given the role based on the assumption that simply because they can teach, they can supervise. In actuality, supervision is composed of a number of observational and interpersonal skills. Burns and Badiali (2016) identified six skills exhibited during the supervision process:

1. noticing (picking up on important aspects of the teaching and learning going on in the lesson observed)
2. pointing (helping the teacher see what the supervisor noticed)
3. ignoring (selectively choosing to disregard some aspects of practice in a hierarchical, triage-like fashion)
4. intervening (getting involved with suggestions for improvement)
5. unpacking (breaking down lesson components for the teacher during the debrief), and
6. processing (facilitating the teacher's reflection on the lesson).

Each occurs during the observation and feedback stages of supervision, and each ultimately needs to be carried out by the teachers on their own.

It is during the post-observation conference where these six processes are mostly enacted with the goal of drawing out teacher reflection. However, researchers like

Farr (2010) found that these conversations contain about 36% teacher talk versus 64% supervisor talk, which also tends to be highly directive. Crasborn et al. (2011) describe this directive style:

> [Supervisors] who use their conversational turns mainly to *bring in* information (i.e. ideas, perspectives, suggestions, feedback, views, instructions) have a more directive supervisory style than [those] who use their conversational turns to *bring out* information, i.e. by asking questions, summarizing aspects of the discussion, and active listening. (p. 321)

If supervisors do not create space for teachers to lead their own self-reflection, then the interactions may not lead to the development of highly reflective practitioners. In fact, as discussed earlier, too often observations are followed by feedback conferences that fall short of teachers' expectations or even cause them to dread being observed (Copland et al., 2009). Therefore, a particular goal of professional development for supervisors is for them to successfully facilitate teacher reflection. Investments in supervisor learning can translate into student learning gains because the more effective supervisors are at observing and providing feedback, the more the process can power teacher learning, in turn impacting learners.

Fanselow (1988) argued that the aims of supervision should be to explore and to see things differently to support teacher noticing, rather than taking over the work of noticing, unpacking, and processing from the teacher. This can only happen, however, if supervisors can explore and see things differently first in their own supervisory practices. Teacher educators and supervisors can demonstrate their engagement with reflection through discussion and dialogue with less experienced colleagues as a means of opening and making visible the process of reflection and encouraging others to do the same. They can also demonstrate this by showing their own teaching, either on-site or through video clips. Fanselow and Hiratsuka (2019, p. 104) talk about this:

> I have always taught classes of practice teachers I observed. If I were a soccer coach, I think I could suggest movements and plays to players that I could not myself do and the players would understand this. Coaches tend to be older than players and less agile. But in the case of teaching, I think we need to try out what we suggest. Teachers can then see that just as they might forget some steps or ignore some students, so do we.
>
> These days when we can record and then jointly view what we both did with the same students, teachers feel more relaxed about seeing

themselves. When I visit a school the second or third time and teach a lesson or part of a lesson both the students and their teachers feel as if what we do is normal, not something special. The teachers see changes I make that are in some ways similar to the ones they make.

Reflective practice can be undermined if teacher educators do not practice what they preach. Brockbank and McGill (2007) argue that academics can only facilitate reflective practice if they themselves use reflection in their own professional development. In fact, Baecher and Kung (2014) found that when presented with a video of teaching, teacher educators realized how little they spend time on reflecting via video artefacts, in spite of the fact that they so often assign teachers to do so. Even when supervisors have access to video, rarely are supervisors brought together in a group to examine the video, discuss, and develop a shared vision of practice, or even calibrate their evaluation tools using a video example. As Bengtsson (2003, p. 295) puts it, this creates a 'paradoxical situation' where reflection can be promoted 'in an unreflected manner'. Edge (2011) too talks of 'consistency' (p. 20) in stating that the demand of teachers that they should be reflective must also be a concomitant demand on supervisors or teacher educators. Edge employs Gore and Zeichner (1991) in making the argument that supervisors cannot simply claim lack of time for being reflective because if they argue that they do not have time, teachers cannot then be blamed for not being reflective about their own teaching.

Like teachers, supervisors benefit greatly from a structured viewing protocol that gives them a focus for looking at their post-observation conferences – in essence, their teaching 'event' as supervisors. And just like teachers who can pull from possible, common foci for ELT observation, supervisors can go to a set of common issues in supervision talk that might give them a viewing target, as presented in Table 7.3.

In the case of the use of video analysis among supervisors, it is important to recognize that the positioning of supervisors as 'experts' may inhibit them from either genuinely believing their practice warrants scrutiny or feeling comfortable openly admitting that their practice could benefit from reflection. Video is effective for creating the cognitive dissonance necessary for supervisors to begin interrogating their own practice and considering how their ideal vision of supervision or their intended actions relate to their actual interactions during supervisory conferences. Viewing their practice alone without having to put it on display or be observed helps experienced supervisors save face and decreases both their sense of vulnerability and their resistance to self-reflection.

In a study carried out by Baecher et al. (2018a), a group of TESOL supervisors gathered in a series of focus groups to share what they found after first engaging individually. Then, they carried out self-reflection by examining videos of their

Table 7.3. Planning the supervisor self-observation

Discussion of the peer-observation process	
Background and goals Consideration of outcomes, concerns, or hesitations for the self-observation. Selection of goals of and focus for the observation*.	What are the learning goals for the supervisor?
Observation data How the supervisor will collect, interpret, and store their observation data, using the observation template.	What types of evidence will the supervisor gather? What protocol will be used?
Logistics Confirmation with the teacher around the logistics of video recording the post-observation session. This may occur live or by recording in a web-conference application.	Which post-observation session will be recorded, and what will the focus be for that conversation?
Impact The conduit and process for enabling the learning to inform wider institutional practices (for example professional learning communities, whole-school instructional practice, curriculum planning).	In what way will the supervisor's self-appraisal relate to school-wide goals? How will the learning be shared with other supervisors?

*7 Focus Area Possibilities Common to Supervisor Observation
(Supervisors can check their own behaviour in these areas).

1. Supervisor Talking Time (TTT) versus Teacher Talking Time
2. Functions of talk (describing, probing, suggesting, evaluating)
3. Organization of talk (opening, topic initiation, closure)
4. Use of data (referring teacher to lesson plan, student work, video of lesson)
5. Use of formulaic talk frames ('compliment sandwich', inauthentic questions)
6. Use of hedging, small talk, tangents to avoid conflict
7. Non-verbal behaviour (eye contact, body positioning)

post-observation sessions. These supervisors arranged to video record a set of post-observation conferences with their teachers, then watched them on their own, taking notes on what they observed in four general phases of the session: opening the session, how they interacted with the teacher, the genre of feedback given, and how they closed the session. The supervisors noticed a variety of aspects of those sessions and came together to share their observations as seen in Table 7.4.

Video, as described above, offers the opportunity for supervisors to self-observe. Using video allows supervisors to 'see' themselves, the way teachers do, in order to trigger the cognitive dissonance needed to help them delve into the gaps between their intentions and their actual behaviours. Because it is a novel practice, there are only a handful of studies so far, but these reveal a number of learning opportunities

Table 7.4. Supervisor insights from video self-observation of conference sessions

Themes	Sample supervisor responses
Opening the POC	'I notice that I ask questions first, about how the teacher thought the lesson went, how they felt about the lesson.'
	'The teacher talks most at the beginning when I ask about how the lesson was for them.'
	'I want to know how the teacher thought the lesson was before I say anything. I was surprised at what they commented on first; it's not what I would have started off with.'
Communication style in the POC	'I thought I gave more praise than I really did. I can see why the teacher might feel insecure after watching how I asked her so many questions.'
	'I noticed that the teacher agrees with everything I say. I now wonder if they just want to get it over with and whether they really understand some of the things I am saying.'
Format of feedback	'I saw myself giving praise and then giving a lot of suggestions.'
	'I asked questions but then I mostly answered them.'
	'I think I might be afraid of letting the teacher talk too much since they sometimes focus on something other than the lesson, and I want to make sure we are staying evidence-based on the lesson.'
Plan for teacher candidate's growth	'At the end of the conversation I notice that I try to review two important areas I want them to make improvements in before we meet again.'
	'I think that the end of the conversation was where I could have let the teacher candidate restate what we had been talking about rather than me going over it for them.'

for supervisors when they review videos of their own feedback sessions, either solo or in a facilitated peer group.

A principal learning gain for supervisors is consciousness-raising about their talk patterns. Vásquez and Reppen (2007) found that when supervisors are conscious of the typical patterns of their talk and work to more actively probe teachers' thinking, they can increase teacher talk significantly. A study by Baecher and Beaumont (2017) promoted self-awareness and led to supervisor discoveries around question-posing that illuminated practices that foster or inhibit teacher talk. Other insights have arisen around the challenges in choosing which moments of the lesson to engage in reflection about with their teachers and in staying with moments of video long enough to generate reflection (Mosley Wetzel et al., 2017).

These insights have also extended to supervisors' turning the camera on the pre-observation lesson planning review session to better understand how to support teacher reasoning during that conference (Pylman, 2016). Supervisors in the ELT field can apply particular foci to their self-observations, such as examining the extent to which their conference talk is generic versus language-specific (Lindahl &

Baecher, 2016), in what ways supervisors interact with first or second language speaking teachers, or how supervisors work to promote critical consciousness around issues of race, gender, and culture with teachers.

One TESOL supervisor who was interested in exploring how she was addressing and challenging teachers she was supervising around asset versus deficit views of English learner students studied her post-observation conferences as the topic of her dissertation research. She collected a series of post-observation conversations with a single teacher, looking at each one through the lens of critical, anti-racist pedagogy. With this inquiry as to her lens, she extracted key moments as a transcript in a dual-entry journal format and shared them with a critical friend, as excerpted in Table 7.5 (Moody, 2020, p. 225).

Table 7.5. Supervisor reflection with critical friend

My findings/interpretations of my post-observation conference talk	Critical friend feedback
I pivoted away from helping K confront biases that she unintentionally raised about her students, instead I validated her challenges and efforts to teach despite the obstacles.	
K expressed frustration with students turning to Spanish to express their ideas, she didn't want them to use it as a crutch and assumed it would hinder them. I didn't notice this bias (L1 interferes with learning L2) and didn't help her unpack it. [K02]	This is the point where I would have opened a discussion about the value of translanguaging and how it promotes acquisition of L2. Then steer the conversation to how to more effectively utilize the skills of L1 to acquire L2.
K assumed a struggling ELL student had a disability although she did acknowledge how the student might not understand her teaching, taking responsibility. I didn't notice her disability assumption and didn't help her unpack it. [K03]	This is when I would interject in a conversation a random statement about noticing the behaviours of several students with no particular focus on the targeted student. Then I would wonder aloud if the targeted student would benefit from some intervention- then either elicit or suggest something specific.
I swept K's deficit thinking under the rug, I didn't notice or challenge her low expectations for students, instead, I guided/facilitated to validate her teaching efforts and facilitate reflection.	
K said her students are 'slow' and I didn't notice or interrogate this negative thinking, which shows low expectations for students, and I only validated her. [K02]	I would have asked K to define slow in this context. Perhaps ask questions about K's ability to speak a second language-I would be subtle of course. Would it have been appropriate to weave in a discussion about differentiation or perhaps the value of re-examining socio-cultural dynamic-pair and group work.
K said her students should have known something (twice) because they were taught it, it shows a 'blame students' mentality. I didn't notice or interrogate this, I only validated her. [K04]	I too sometimes fall into a situation when I find myself validating a teacher's negative comments. It is one thing to acknowledge the negative comments and another to validate them. What language patterns have you internalized?

Supervisors independently looking at their own feedback sessions parallels teachers looking at their own videos of practice for the purpose of self-appraisal. Among teachers, peer observation has numerous benefits for teacher learning, supervisor collaborative peer inquiry can also be beneficial to supervisor learning, although peer inquiry is not typically found between supervisors. As with teachers looking at their practice in peer groups, supervisors will benefit and feel safer to fully engage if the process is facilitated and structured. In Baecher and Beaumont (2017), a protocol is suggested for engaging supervisors in peer observation and peer feedback, which could be adapted based on local interest or purposes, outlined in Table 7.6.

More than 50 years ago, Goldhammer (1969) emphasized the need for supervision to become a tool in enabling teachers to understand what they are doing and why by changing schools from places where teachers just act out age-old rituals to places where teachers participate fully in their own professional growth. With video, so much is possible; teachers and supervisors alike can engage in ongoing self-observation and have access to peers' practice both near and far. However, thoughtful

Table 7.6. Protocol for supervisor video-based peer observation

Step 1.	**Supervisors opt in to reviewing their practice with a trusted colleague or group of supervisors:** A focus for their review of video is established along with a common vocabulary about feedback sessions and goals for the process.
Step 2	**Supervisor video analysis with protocol:** Supervisors review, on their own, a video recording of a post-observation conference, using a structured viewing guide to collect data and organize findings based on chosen focus. Descriptive rather than judgemental notes are taken as much as possible.
Step 3	**Collaborative conversation with peer supervisor:** Supervisors share video with a trusted peer(s) who will act as a critical friend in the inquiry process. Peer supervisors review the video and mark with time-stamps, moments to bring up for discussion based on the supervisors' stated interest. They meet in person or online and discuss the conference.
Step 4	**Analysis of the post-observation conference:** Questions explored are brought up related to the supervisors' focus area and others that might foster discussion of philosophical underpinnings and stances, such as: 1. Describe the type of supervisor or supervisory practice you are shooting for. 2. Did you have a goal or planned trajectory of some kind in this interaction? 3. How clear is your language? What would the teacher candidate walk away remembering from this conference? 4. If there is a model here for supervisors, what parts of the model are tied to you and your personality or expertise? Which are teachable to other supervisors? 5. What do you see related to your use of silence or wait time?
Step 5	**Determining next steps:** Like in teacher supervision, supervisors can decide how they want to experiment with their practice and continue to evolve their skills in facilitating teacher learning.

processes and protocols must be provided in order for participants to feel they are learning in non-threatening ways. We continue to understand more about the complexity and sensitivity required in the mediation that takes place in supervisory conversations. As Waring (2013) states, 'there is no doubt that much of this enterprise hinges...upon mentors' ability to create a space that allows for the open sharing of teacher perspectives' (p. 105).

Video can provide an opportunity for these key players – supervisors, coaches, trainers, and teachers – to gain direct insight into their practice. Video analysis can be instrumental in bringing the teacher and coach/supervisor together to build a shared vision, grounded in the evidence that can be seen and discussed in video review.

Reflective Break

1. If you are currently providing feedback to teachers, what do you see as your strengths, challenges, or potential blind spots in the supervision, coaching, or feedback you give? How might the introduction of video review impact your current experience supervising?
2. What are the opportunities and obstacles in your context for introducing video into supervision?
3. Which of the suggested activities seem most do-able for you and other teachers at your site?

Chapter 8
Video in Research

INTRODUCTION

This final chapter offers a review of the ways in which video can be employed and conceptualized in TESOL and Applied Linguistics research. As discussed in previous chapters, the availability of digital video has not only changed how educators communicate and learn about teaching, but also how research is conducted. This chapter explores the role of video in capturing data from complex classroom interactions and recording informant experience and beliefs vital to research. Video has become a popular data collection tool for those undertaking educational research, offering a resource that can be very helpful in pinning down temporal aspects, activities, and sequences of events. It offers a fine-grained record of the ecology of a classroom which can be reused, re-edited, and shared. We also look at how video tools and software can help researchers investigate language teaching, student learning, and teacher education and development.

This chapter examines four ways in which research and the research community have benefited from video: collecting video data for research purposes, the use of video-stimulated recall research, new technologies for using video in research, and the dissemination of research findings via video. Even those who are not direct consumers or producers of research per se will find these approaches, analytic tools, and methodologies applicable to classroom reflection.

COLLECTING VIDEO DATA FOR RESEARCH PURPOSES

Each of the chapters in the book up to now has included citations and quotations about the use of video from relevant studies; we have included research into the effectiveness of video use in developing greater awareness of classroom interaction, studies on how video expands teaching options and shared empirical links between video review and reflective practice. Here we focus on how video is used as a tool in gathering data for research, rather than training, purposes.

Researchers in TESOL and Applied Linguistics are employing video data to answer a variety of research questions. In doing this, they draw on concepts and methodology in the fields of multimodality (e.g., Kress, 2010), the related fields of video ethnography and linguistic ethnography (e.g., Graesch et al., 2006), and participatory action research researchers.

Linguistic ethnography as a research field has placed particular value on the collection and analysis of video for fine-grained analysis. Sometimes this is in combination with field notes, and sometimes instead of face-to-face site visits. Especially in research that spans international and diverse sites, using informants to collect video has become more common. After all, it is often too expensive and time-consuming to visit research sites face to face. Linguistic ethnography has been at the centre of efforts to use video to consider ideology, power, structure and agency, voice, identity, social change, and diversity. In pursuit of these themes, video plays an important role in working towards a commitment to detailed documentation and analysis of social action, interaction, and human artefacts. As Bezemer and Abdullahi (2019, p. 125) explain:

> This translates into a stance that is about the appreciation of 'smallness and slowness' (Silverman, 1999, who attributes this phrase to Harvey Sacks); and a preference for the use of materials that afford such fine-grained analysis, e.g. digital (video) recordings.

Researchers of multimodality also naturally gravitate to the use of video as a multimodal data collection instrument. While video has the potential to capture detailed, fine-grained interaction it also can capture broad contextual features, as Jewitt explains:

> Well, most people who work with a multimodal perspective collect video and data. And that's because it's practically impossible to collect the detail of data that you need to do a multimodal analysis using notes. But some people do use those notes and supplement that with photographs of interaction. I prominently use video. And that means having the sense beforehand of exactly what kind of interaction you need to capture. So sometimes, with the use of video, it's the pay-off between the real detail of the interaction, like close-up interaction you might need, and getting a broader view as well as of the kind of

context of the interaction. (https://methods.sagepub.com/video/multimodal-research-jewitt)

In the collection of video data, participatory video approaches have also become more prominent, especially with the increased use of interventionist and collaborative ways of researching (e.g., action research and exploratory practice). Some of this work has adopted methodology from community activism, international development, health, and social work, as well as environmental sustainability projects. Participatory ways of working with video seek to bridge the gap between the theories, models, and concepts of researchers and those of individual teachers, students, and parents (Edge, 2011). In many cases, there is an element of giving control of the video camera over to the participants to document their learning and experiences as a clear expression of the research team's desire to create parity with participants. The use of video diaries or vlogging has also helped make research projects more collaborative and participatory. There has been interesting recent work on getting students involved in vlog use (e.g., Taqwa & Sandi, 2019) and this has become a collaborative option for data collection. Participatory video research aims to 'reduce the gap between the concepts and models of researchers and those of individuals and communities' (Jewitt, 2012, p. 3). This often involves participants being provided with access to, and training in, the use of video-recording equipment. This generates three kinds of video-related data:

1. the video 'as product',
2. the process of its production – which itself is often video-recorded,
3. the process of video editing.

These overlapping forms of video data become the focus of further exploration and study, although some participatory video research prioritizes one over the other, or may emphasize the interaction between them (Jewitt, 2012). As educational research looks for more participatory mechanisms for involving and collaborating with researchers, we have witnessed greater use of classroom interaction-based teacher education frameworks, including SETT (Walsh, 2006, 2011), IMDAT (Sert, 2015) and the British Council Video-Based Observation scheme (Borg, 2021).

Hennessy (2014) provides examples of how dialogue with researchers, stimulated by the video material, led to teachers formulating their craft knowledge in more theoretical terms. This then contributed to the generation of codes in the analytical process and development towards greater knowledge in teaching. The claim is that such video-related dialogue can play a developmental role for both teachers and researchers (see Nind et al., 2015 for similar experiences and examples).

Usually, video data is one form of data. Morton (2019, pp. 174–175) refers in the following example to different stages of data collection, showing how each data collection cycle feeds into the next stage.

> Data were collected at three stages, each relating to one of the components of the tripartite view of language knowledge. To focus on language as a curricular concern, the teachers filled in an instrument called a Content Representation...in which they identified the key concepts and language features they planned to focus on in a topic they were about to teach. This document was used as the basis of a semi-structured interview, in which the teachers were able to reflect on their planning processes, particularly how language issues fitted into their view of the curriculum they were teaching. In order to focus on language as a tool for learning, for each teacher, three lessons were videorecorded. Using a modified stimulated recall technique, brief clips in which issues discussed in the previous interviews emerged, or incidents that brought into sharp relief aspects of language as a tool for learning, were presented to the teachers for comment. The teachers' representations of language as a matter of competence (their students' or their own) emerged in both the pre- and post-teaching interviews and were also evidenced in the classroom interaction data.

Teachers doing action research often use videos as a tool for self-reflection, and a collection of such teacher action research projects using video can be found in Rebolledo et al. (2018). In these cases, teachers use devices they have at hand to self-record one or more lessons, which they then watch for reflection and analysis. Since these teachers work with mentors in their projects, together they create protocols to focus on the aspects that are relevant for their individual action research projects.

While the most common form of data collection via video is simply recording lessons, it is important to note the use of video data from interviews as well as video surveys (Stigler et al., 2000). Increasingly, video is captured and then used in more than one way within a research project in a mixed-methods approach that can potentially draw on large quantities of video data for indexing and retrieval:

> Quantitative analyses are rendered more interpretable by being efficiently linked to specific video examples of the categories coded. The key enabler for this kind of research has been the revolution in multimedia computer technology over the past 5 years. Now it is possible to

archive large quantities of video information in a way that can easily be indexed and retrieved. (Stigler et al., 2000, p. 87)

Reflective Break
1. If you are a researcher, how have you used video data in your studies? How might you further explore video data?
2. If you carry out teacher action research projects, how might video data be captured and then analysed? Could students be involved as videographers?
3. What are the drawbacks and strengths of using video data in research?
4. What kind of ethical considerations do researchers need to address in their projects?

VIDEO-STIMULATED RECALL RESEARCH

While all of the types of research that utilize video as data described above involve close analysis of the video record, a particular approach to this analysis uses video as both data and method. At its best, stimulated recall methodology using video records involves the researcher and the research participant working in tandem to co-construct a view of what has happened. Each brings a different perspective, and the insider and outsider reach an understanding of what they view. Sometimes it might be the researcher that pauses the video to elicit a 'what's going on here?' question or prompt; on other occasions, the participant is encouraged to pause the video and try to recover their thinking. This 're-entering the moment' can provide insights into what happened during the lessons and related reflections.

Video-stimulated recall interviewing established itself as a widely used methodological tool in educational research (Jones et al., 2009). It is particularly helpful in comparing espoused beliefs with beliefs-in-action (Rosaen et al., 2008). It is also valuable for getting insights into teacher cognition and thinking behind teacher action. Sometimes these insights are unexpected and lead the researcher into new areas of analysis. Claudia Bustos (personal communication) talking about her research on mentor training in Chile says that:

Video-stimulated recall offered access to much richer data. Asking my participants to choose bits of their mentor-mentee conferences allowed them to also have an agenda in the interview, which expanded the conversation to areas that I might have not seen otherwise.

If you have not seen this process, it might be helpful to observe it in action. In this video (https://vilte.warwick.ac.uk/items/show/43) we see a session where Jason (the researcher) is working with a teacher (Fred). This is a good example of what can be achieved with these techniques: Jason attempts to recover Fred's thoughts within the moments and episodes captured (rather than his current observations, general beliefs, or post-hoc rationalization). Jason also suggests that 'the advantage of the method used is that it gives control of the playback to the teacher participant, reducing both the pressure to need to recall and the danger of the teacher second-guessing the researcher's interest or intent if the latter has control of playback' (see also Hidson, 2018). Such a process can provide insight into some of the real-time choices and decisions that teachers make as they tweak their teaching, and adjust and scaffold learning (Schepens et al., 2007). Jason takes us through this thinking in the following vignette.

Vignette: Video-Stimulated Recall
Jason Anderson
University of Warwick

Video-stimulated recall (VSR) is an important tool for researchers interested in investigating aspects of teacher cognition, particularly where the aim is to understand more about areas such as decision making, improvisation, and classroom management. I made use of VSR in a research project in which my aim was to document and then analyse examples of teacher reflection-in-action (see Anderson, 2019), a construct developed by Donald Schön (1983).

After a pilot study to try out and refine the method, the main study involved four teachers in two phases typical for VSR: lesson recording and recall recording. During lesson recording, two lessons of each teacher were video-recorded after an initial observation to acclimatise learners and teacher to the presence of researcher and camera in the classroom. The camera was placed in an unobtrusive spot at the back of the classroom, facing the teacher and also showing the board and some of the learners. I sat next to it and made notes of lesson events of importance to my research aims.

Recall recording happened immediately after the lesson. This was essential to preserve as much as possible of the teacher's recollections of their interactive thought. I quickly transferred the lesson video recording to a laptop computer. The teacher then sat in front of this computer and was given control of playback. I also projected the lesson they were watching to a second monitor (via HDMI) and set up a video camera to capture both of these simultaneously.

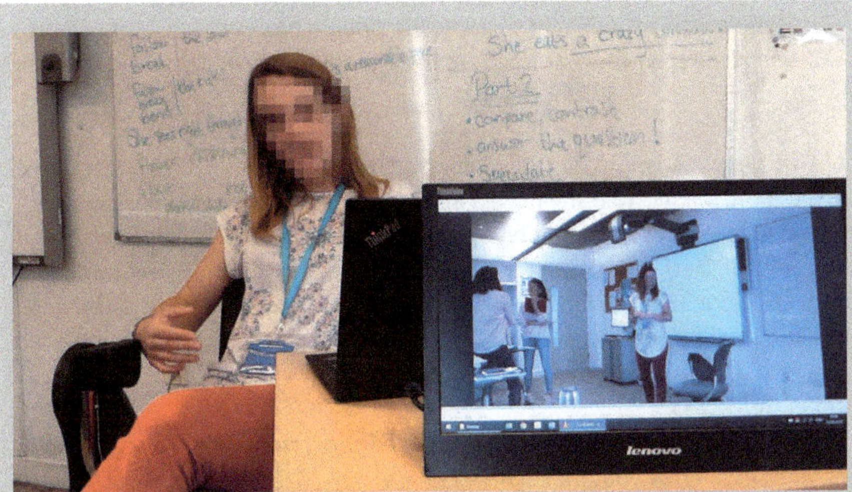

Figure 8.1. Still photo of teacher reviewing their video of practice

Figure 8.1 shows a teacher participating in video-stimulated recall, with a still shot from the recall camera showing both the original lesson and the teacher's response during playback.

Capturing the video itself and the teachers recall on one screen avoided needing to resync the two videos afterwards. The teacher was asked to play certain sections of the lesson and to pause playback and verbalise recollections whenever they could remember their thoughts and concerns at the moment in question 'including things you noticed, things you felt, decision moments, reflections, confusions, problems, etc.' (Anderson, 2019, pp. 4–5). The recall camera thus captured the lesson events, the teacher's recall comments, and also their paralinguistic response during recall, which was also useful to the research aims. Recall recording lasted 50–70 minutes and finished with each teacher reflecting on the VSR process itself.

Afterwards, both lesson and recall sessions were transcribed and analysed, first to develop a typology of interactive thought, and then to identify and categorise reflective episodes, which were triangulated with other data sources (e.g., audio diaries, initial interviews, lesson plans), enabling me to hypothesise on the extent to which each episode involved more automated, or more consciously deliberated thought that may have been formative, consistent with Schön's construct.

Evidence suggests that the process used was generally successful in enabling participant teachers to recall their interactive thoughts. Three of the four participants felt it was comparatively easy to do:

I was quite able to um, to get back into my thought processes um from all the segments that we looked at and I found it quite easy to do that (Anderson, 2019, p. 6).

The fourth had more difficulty, reflected in fewer recalls. This was likely due to the more passive role she played in large parts of her two lessons, which involved extensive reading and writing skills work when her role was minimal. I was also satisfied with the outcome of the process, given the significant technical and cognitive challenges involved; the pilot study had been essential in fine-tuning this process.

Reflective Break
1. In what situations might video-stimulated conversation take place either in your research or your practice?
2. If you carry out teacher action research projects, how might video data be captured and then analysed? Could students be involved as videographers?

TECHNOLOGIES FOR USING VIDEO IN RESEARCH

New technologies both help shape the way we can work with video but also the nature of the actual video we are able to secure and what we might do with that video. Two technologies, in particular, virtual reality/360° video and sophisticated annotation tools, have transformed how classrooms can be viewed and are widely available.

Like using video data obtained by multiple camera sources (Kilburn, 2014), the use of virtual reality (VR) and '360° videos' has the potential to amplify what can be viewed from a single camera (Mann et al., 2019). Driver (2017) and Walshe and Driver (2019) have recently started to explore the value of VR as the increasing use of tools like Google Cardboard (https://arvr.google.com/cardboard/) in classrooms is helping to raise interest in this possibility. Rather than just focusing on the teacher at the front, 360° video allows more to be captured than single lens video and can help teachers and researchers to become more conscious of teaching context and situated learning. This also enables a more extensive set of data to be generated to focus on classroom behaviours, interaction and embodied interaction (Snelson & Hsu, 2019). In an interview for the ViLTE project on 360°, a teacher says 'it's totally different. When you are observing classes through virtual reality, you're immersed in the context. You feel like, as a student, you have the possibility of turning around and observing what's going on behind you or next to you'.

Case studies can be developed that include 360° video, such as Goff's from OnVu Learning (https://www.onvulearning.com/school-case-studies/), and used for teachers to share clips with colleagues and mentors as part of ongoing professional development or be tapped into for research into classroom practice. Windscheid and Will (2018) also use 360° video in their programme VideoLeB (http://www. videoleb.de/) allows teachers or researchers to have a more immersive experience and more control in being able to make decisions about what to view, what to focus on and what to take notes about as they can be tagged to particular moments in the video and are therefore more easily shared or discussed with peers. In order to give viewers more choices in watching and analysing the video content, they developed a synchronized multi-screen 360° video player. This has additional features for video analysis (e.g., timestamp, an annotation marker), and the 360° video player can display up to three videos synchronously, although each video can also be viewed in full-screen mode (watch https://www.youtube.com/watch?v=Ia_hAXGR0Yo for an introduction to VideoLeb on YouTube).

Video annotation is much easier and more systematic with increasingly sophisticated analytic tools. Software such as NviVo, Transana, MaxQDA, Videograph, or StudioCode allows researchers a multimodal interface for repeated viewing, connecting episodes to notes, transcripts, and other artefacts. Different data sets can be interconnected, making multiple coding easier to accomplish (Stigler et al., 2000). Heath et al. (2010) and Xu et al. (2018) provide practical guidance on the use of video qualitative video-based studies of a wide range of organizational environments. There have also been important contributions to video annotation in the DIVER (diver.stanford.edu), and Constellations (orion.njit.edu) projects.

Tools like Transana https://www.youtube.com/watch?v=Y2D0Ph-Zots (see also Mavrou et al., 2007; CraigRush, 2019) present video in a multimedia interface in which associated annotations and metadata such as tags, captions, subtitles, labels, hyperlinks, data about gaze, proxemics are readily accessible for collaborative analysis and discussion.

Vignette: Video Software for Analytic Purposes
Olcay Sert
Mälardalen University, Sweden

I am a researcher of classroom interaction and English language teacher education whose work also involves observing, examining, and teaching student teachers. Video is central to my research, as well as to my teaching. In this short vignette, I will introduce two different pieces of video software, *Transana* and *Wondershare Filmora*. I use the former for analytic purposes during my research,

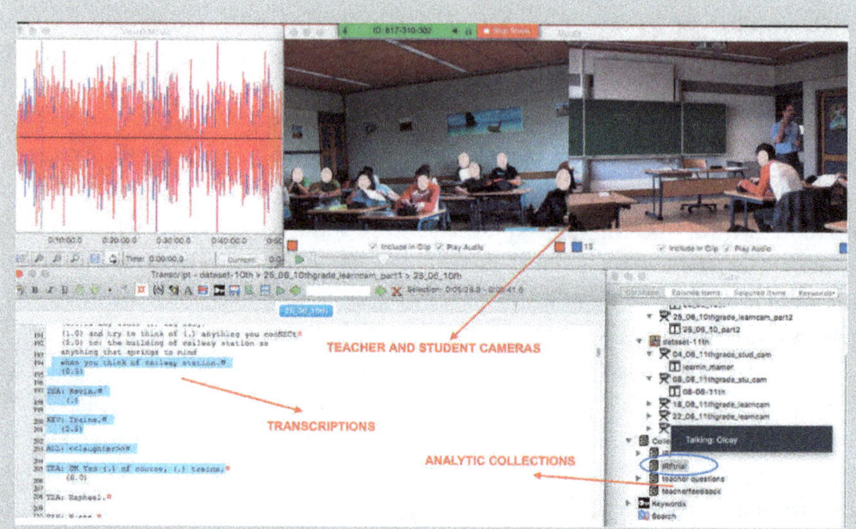

Figure 8.2. Transana interface: an EFL classroom in Luxembourg

while the latter is a video-editing tool that aids in transforming my research find-ings into video materials that I use in teacher education.

I use Transana to analyse video and audio data that come from classrooms and post-observation feedback sessions. Transana enables me to synchronize multiple data sources (e.g., digital recordings from two cameras that focus on the teacher and the learners separately, as in the top-right of Figure 8.2), and align my transcriptions (bottom-left) and collections (bottom-right) with mo-ments in lessons.

After I collect video data, I first upload the recordings to Transana, and syn-chronize the data sources using the sound waves on the top-left of Figure 8.2. I then start transcribing the data and assign time codes to utterances. Assigning time codes to the transcriptions aligns the video and the transcription, which eventually helps me build collections of interactional and pedagogical phe-nomena. For instance, I can simply drag and drop each instance of a correction from a teacher to the collection labels that I create on the bottom-right of the screen. My collections built bottom-up, become the bases of my research find-ings, which I then use to write research articles and presentations in academic conferences.

In the past, I used Transana and selected video excerpts from the collections during my presentations and classes. However, I felt the need to annotate se-lected video excerpts, because the Transana interface was not ideal for presen-tations and teaching. The detailed transcriptions were distracting and difficult

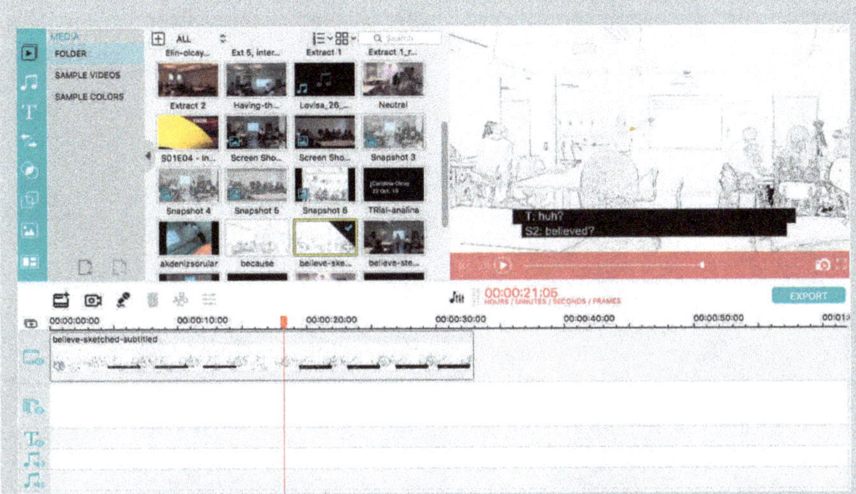

Figure 8.3. Wondershare Filmora user interface

to follow, and I needed visual annotations on the video to emphasize pedagogical and interactional phenomena. Furthermore, and even more importantly, I had to anonymize some of the videos to protect students' and teachers' identity.

Wondershare Filmora has so far been able to help me in addressing these problems and I have been using it in the last few years to use my video extracts in presentations and to highlight pedagogical aspects of interaction during my teaching and workshops for (student) teachers. *Filmora* has a user-friendly interface (Figure 8.3) that has allowed me to sketch or anonymize videos using a variety of filters, add subtitles and texts on videos, and annotate videos by adding comment balloons, images, and shapes.

Figure 8.4 shows a black & white sketch filter I used to anonymize participants. The utterances of the teachers and students can be represented in a variety of ways. In this example, I was focusing on instructions, and I was able to highlight parts of the transcripts in a different colour, in this case, red.

Filmora is especially useful for visual annotations, and I have found that in my workshops, classes, and presentations, organization of the foci of the video helps the audience notice important aspects of teaching and learning events. In Figure 8.5, for example, the focal participant in the video was highlighted with a red oval and her utterance was transcribed and added to the video. Her gaze direction was represented with a white arrow, while what she sees on the board was also added (bottom) to the video as a separate layer (see Sert, 2019) for more visuals and analyses).

Figure 8.4. A video sketched using Filmora: a Swedish EFL classroom

Figure 8.5. A screenshot from a video annotated using Filmora

Such videos that I edited using Filmora have been found to be useful by especially student teachers and teachers who are not familiar with advanced transcriptions in research publications. I use a collaborative discovery method to implement these materials in my teaching. The method involves first viewing a video (and accompanying transcriptions where relevant) with 2 or 3 open questions given by me, then working briefly in groups to discuss phenomena observed in the video, and finally reporting the perspectives that emerge from group discussions.

It is a challenge to be a researcher and a teacher educator at the same time, as these two identities may sometimes be at odds. However, I believe that research and teacher education should go hand-in-hand and inform each other. As I argued elsewhere (Sert, 2010, 2013) *Transana* is primarily a research software, but it can be a useful tool for us to present analytic findings too. However, in order to 'transform conversation analytic findings into future teaching practices' (Sert, 2020), we may need tools like *Filmora* that afford multimodal annotations on video materials for teachers, students, and trainees. These two software programs, I argue, are complementary and for a researcher who is a teacher educator at the same time, they aid in the communication of research findings to practitioners.

Reflective Break

1. What possibilities do you see for the use of 360° video for teacher learning or for research? Is it something that could offer more than what you are currently able to view?
2. Have you ever tried annotating video for a research project? What approaches have you implemented, and what are their benefits and challenges?

VIDEO AS A TOOL IN THE DISSEMINATION OF RESEARCH

As we have seen throughout this book, researchers in TESOL, Education, and Applied Linguistics have studied their work with video analysis and published these findings. However, one of the difficulties reported by teachers, graduate students, and researchers is accessing research findings due to a lack of access to primary research papers which are unavailable behind paywalls. One element of making their work more relevant and accessible is to make it available in video format. To make research more accessible, some journals are encouraging researchers to make their work available video in the form of brief webinars (e.g. https://academic.oup.com/eltj/pages/editors_choice_videos).

For instance, Jarvis' website *TESOL Academic* (https://www.tesolacademic.org/) recognized the barriers to access to research in the field of TESOL many years ago and uses their website to bring research findings directly to English language teachers. Jarvis (in Mann et al., 2019, p. 34) asks the researchers to discuss and explain their research in video format. Jarvis describes his drive to create this repository:

> I think there was a sense in which my gut feeling was that if you see
> people, even if it is in a YouTube video, rather than a face-to-face
> meeting, you can see people talking about their work. You get a sense
> of the passion that they have and you get a sense of what drives them.
> Also, you've got the kind of paralinguistic stuff going on. You can see
> it and that's missing when you read their books and their publications,
> those books can sometimes be quite dry.

Video can be particularly engaging for teachers who either do not have access to a range of journals or who might find this kind of written format hard to engage with. Many leading academics are featured on Jarvis' website and there are over 60 talks on either articles or books, and this project is documented in Jarvis (2017) 'TESOLacademic.org: Our Ever Changing Story'.

Another important function of video in the research community is to meet the needs of those who are interested in gaining insights into researchers' theoretical approach and also want to learn more about the research steps and procedures. Videos are widely available which walk through methodological approaches. The SAGE website (https://methods.sagepub.com/video), for instance, is particularly helpful as it is searchable by discipline and university-based 'research methods' modules. Table 8.1 provides an overview of resources that offer research and research methods for those who are interested in exploring or joining the research community using video as a means for engagement.

Making video versions of research findings and outcomes increases engagement with a wide group of potential users and increases the chance of impact. For example, the UK Research and Innovation brings together the UK's seven research councils, Innovate UK and Research England to maximize the contribution of each council and create the best environment for research and innovation to flourish. ESRC and EU funding increasingly depends on innovative and engaging ways to communicate research to increase the impact and visibility of research.

It is now a requirement that the research project outcomes need to be disseminated to a wide-ranging audience through multiple channels, e.g., video, research articles, webpages, photo exhibitions, books, drama productions. Video dissemination can increase and improve the social and educational impact of research. Although the ViLTE project (Mann et al., 2019) produced a written research report, the main resource, where informants produced videos that made their ways of working with video visible, was the repository of videos (https://vilte.warwick.ac.uk/). It was always an important element of the design to ultimately produce this kind of video resource.

Table 8.1. Research and research methods presented through video

Title	About	Link
The International Festival of Teacher Research in ELT conferences	This website hosts 'Festival outputs' in the form of video recordings of presentations at the events. They have been made available to broaden access to teachers in 'developing countries, in particular, who may not otherwise have access to professional development opportunities of the kind envisaged'. In the videos, researchers give practical and theoretical insight into carrying out teacher research.	https://trfestival.wordpress.com/
We Share Science	*We Share Science* is a place that people can share, search, and discuss today's research. They host research abstracts and researcher interviewers.	https://wesharescience.com/ (There is not an area specifically dedicated to our field but does have videos in the education section e.g., https://wesharescience.com/pin/4546 and https://wesharescience.com/pin/5540.)
SAGE videos	On the SAGE webpage, there is a section on research methods called SAGE Research Methods Video. This provides hundreds of video titles showing research in action to help users build their skills as they prepare to conduct original research.	https://us.sagepub.com/en-us/nam/sage-video
Research Methods in Linguistics and Applied Linguistics	This website provides materials and videos on research design, data analysis, and statistics.	https://appliedlinguistics.org.uk/
TESOLacademic	This YouTube channel supports the work of the Teaching English to Speakers of Other Languages (TESOL) academic website and that of Huw Jarvis. It is a free-at-source collection of 24 'Keynotes' and 46 'Research Paper' videos.	https://www.youtube.com/user/TESOLacademic/videos
Welcome to The ELT Research Garage	This site hosts short videos of the papers the host has published to disseminate the findings and practical implications that teachers could use as well as researchers talking about their work and guidance on how to write a conference abstract.	https://www.youtube.com/channel/UCnMTK06gmce2zXxXLojc1XQ
Academic English Now	This YouTube channel aims to provide writing advice for students and researchers. The host's videos are 'how to…' in style, for example how to write an introduction, how to write a research proposal etc.	https://www.youtube.com/channel/UChKdxjtlyaS21ZuCdpL9ahA

As seen in this chapter, researchers in education and applied linguistics increasingly recognize that video is a powerful medium for communicating with a wide audience. Video can help ensure both engagement and impact.

References

Admiraal, W., Janssen, T., Huizenga, J., Kranenburg, F., Taconis, R., & Corda, A. (2014). E-assessment of student-teachers' competence as new teachers. *Turkish Online Journal of Educational Technology, 13*(4), 21–29.

Akcan, S. (2010). Watching teacher candidates watch themselves: Reflections on a practicum program in Turkey. *Profile Issues in Teachers Professional Development, 12*(1), 33–45.

Alles, M., Seidel, T., & Gröschner, A. (2019). Establishing a positive learning atmosphere and conversation culture in the context of a video-based teacher learning community. *Professional Development in Education, 45*(2), 250–263.

Ally, M., Grimus, M., & Ebner, M. (2014). Preparing teachers for a mobile world, to improve access to education. *Prospects, 44*(1), 43–59.

Almingefeldt, E. (2019a). Filmed oral examinations [Conference paper]. Nästa Generations Lärande (Next Generation Teaching) (NGL2019) University of Dalarna, October 16, 2020, https://www.du.se/ngl2019.

Almingefeldt, E. (2019b). Filmed oral examinations – why are not all teachers doing this? [Conference film] Symposium: Praxis in higher education – with a focus on the Nordic context, University of Borås May 22–24, 2019, https://youtu.be/pOfoJjyjy-8.

Anderson, J. (2019). In search of reflection-in-action. *Teaching and Teacher Education, 86*, 1–17. https://0-doi-org.pugwash.lib.warwick.ac.uk/10.1016/j.tate.2019.102879

Angelides, P. (2001). The development of an efficient technique for collecting and analyzing qualitative data: The analysis of critical incidents. *International Journal of Qualitative Studies in Education, 14*, 429–442.

Arthur, L., Marland, H., Pill, A., & Rea, T. (2010). School culture and postgraduate professional development: Delineating the 'enabling school'. *Professional Development in Education, 36*(3), 471–489.

Asanok, M., & Chookhampaeng, C. (2016). Coaching and mentoring model based on teachers' professional development for enhancing their teaching competency in schools (Thailand) using video tape. *Educational Research and Reviews, 11*(4), 134–140.

Bacova, D., Rodriguez-Yborra, M., & Booth, E. (2016). *First steps to teaching: A handbook.* https://warwick.ac.uk/fac/soc/al/research/vilte/resources/first_steps_to_teaching_dvd_booklet.pdf

Baecher, L. (2019). *Video in teacher learning: Through their own eyes*. Corwin.

Baecher, L., & Beaumont, J. (2017). Supervisor reflection for teacher education: Video-based inquiry as model. *The European Journal of Applied Linguistics, 6*(2), 65–84.

Baecher, L., & Kung, S. C. (2011). Jumpstarting novice teachers' ability to analyze classroom video: Affordances of an online workshop. *Journal of Digital Learning in Teacher Education, 28*(1), 16–26.

Baecher, L., & Kung, S. C. (2014). Collaborative video inquiry as teacher educator professional development. *Issues in Teacher Education, 22*(2), 93–115.

Baecher, L., & McCormack, B. (2012). Clinical supervision as opportunity for self-study. In *Proceedings of the Ninth International Conference on Self-Study of Teacher Education Practices* (pp. 164–168). Brigham Young University.

Baecher, L., & McCormack, B. (2015). The impact of video review on supervisory conferencing. *Language and Education, 29*(2), 153–173.

Baecher, L., Graves, S. & Ghailan, F. (2018a). Supervisor learning through collaborative video inquiry: It's not just for teacher candidates. *Contemporary Issues in Technology and Teacher Education, 18*(3).

Baecher, L., Kung, S. C., Ward, S. L., & Kern, K. (2018b). Facilitating video analysis for teacher development: A systematic review of the research. *Journal of Technology and Teacher Education, 26*(2), 185–216.

Baker, K. (2020, May 18). Covid-19 is changing education for the better. *Financial Times*. Retrieved February 27, 2022, from https://www.ft.com/content/51496fde-98e7-11ea-871b-edeb99a20c6e

Barahona, M. (2019). What matters to supervisors and is this reflected in what they do? Analysing the work of university supervisors of the practicum. *Journal of Education for Teaching, 45*(3), 262–276.

Bates, M. S., Phalen, L., & Moran, C. G. (2016). If you build it, will they reflect? Examining teachers' use of an online video-based learning website. *Teaching and Teacher Education, 58*, 17–27.

Batlle, J., & P. Miller. (2017). *Video enhanced observation and teacher development: Teachers' beliefs as technology users*. In *EDULEARN17 Proceedings*: 9th International Conference on Education and New Learning Technologies, Valencia: IATED.

Batlle, J., & Seedhouse, P. (2021). Integrating the Video Enhanced Observation (VEO) app in peer observation feedback interaction. In Seedhouse, P. (Ed.) *Video Enhanced Observation for Language Teaching*. Bloomsbury.

Bauer, R., Meissl-Egghart, G., Vohle, F., & Szucsich, P. (2019). How to encourage reflective practice with the help of collaborative video annotation: Social video learning in teacher education. In A. Reid (Ed.), *Marginalia in modern learning contexts* (pp. 133–165). IGI Global.

Bayram, L. (2012). Use of online video cases in teacher training. *Procedia-Social and Behavioral Sciences, 47*, 1007–1011.

Bengtsson, J. (2003). Possibilities and limits of self-reflection in the teaching profession. *Studies in Philosophy and Education, 22*(3–4), 295–316.

Benitt, N. (2019). Campus meets classroom: Video conferencing and reflective practice in language teacher education. *European Journal of Applied Linguistics and TEFL, 8*(2), 121–139.

Bezemer, J., & Abdullahi, S. (2019). Multimodality. In K. Tusting (Ed.), *The Routledge handbook of linguistic ethnography* (pp. 125–157). Routledge.

Blijleven, P. (2005). *Multimedia-cases: Towards a bridge between theory and practice.* Unpublished doctoral dissertation, University of Twente, The Netherlands.

Blomberg, G., Sherin, M. G., Renkl, A., Glogger, I., & Seidel, T. (2014). Understanding video as a tool for teacher education: Investigating instructional strategies to promote reflection. *Instructional Science, 42*(3), 443–463.

Borg, S. (2015). *Teacher cognition and language education: Research and practice.* Bloomsbury.

Borg, S., Lightfoot, A., & Gholkar, R. (2020). *Professional development through teacher activity groups.* https://www.teachingenglish.org.uk/sites/teacheng/files/TAG_review_final_web.pdf

Borko, H., Jacobs, J., Eiteljorg, E., & Pittman, M. E. (2008). Video as a tool for fostering productive discussions in mathematics professional development. *Teaching and Teacher Education, 24,* 417–436.

Bozbıyık, M. (2017). *The implementation of VEO in an English language education context: A focus on teacher questioning practices.* (Unpublished master's thesis). Gazi University, Ankara. https://warwick.ac.uk/fac/soc/al/research/vilte/resources/merve_bozbiyik_ma_thesis.pdf

Brockbank, A., & McGill, I. (2007). *Facilitating reflective learning in higher education.* McGraw-Hill Education.

Brophy, J. (2004). *Using video in teacher education.* Elsevier.

Brouwer, N. (2007). *Imaging teacher learning: A literature review on the use of digital video for preservice teacher education and teacher professionalization.* ILS Graduate School of Education.

Brouwer, N. (2011). *Imaging teacher learning: A review on the use of digital video for preservice teacher education and professional development.* Paper presented at the Annual Meeting of the American Educational Research Association, New Orleans, LA.

Brunvand, S., & Fishman, B. (2006). Investigating the impact of the availability of scaffolds on preservice teacher noticing and learning from video. *Journal of Educational Technology Systems, 35*(2), 151–174.

Burns, R. W., & Badiali, B. (2016). Unearthing the complexities of clinical pedagogy in supervision: Identifying the pedagogical skills of supervisors. *Action in Teacher Education, 38*(2), 156–174.

Calandra, B., Brantley-Dias, L., Lee, J. K., & Fox, D. L. (2009). Using video editing to cultivate novice teachers' practice. *Journal of Research on Technology in Education, 42*(1), 73–94.

Calandra, B., Brantley-Dias, L., Yerby, J., & Demir, K. (2018). Examining the quality of preservice science teachers' written reflections when using video recordings, audio recordings, and memories of a teaching event. *Contemporary Issues in Technology and Teacher Education, 18*(1), 81–101.

Calvani, A., Bonaiuti, G., & Andreocci, B. (2011). Il microteaching rinascerà a nuova vita? Video annotazione e sviluppo della riflessività del docente. Available at https://iris.unica.it/retrieve/handle/11584/31580/177795/2011%20SIRD%20029-044calvani.pdf

Carlson, S., & Gadio, C. T. (2002). Teacher professional development in the use of technology. In W. D. Haddad & A. Draxler (Eds.), *Technologies for education: Potentials, parameters, and prospects.* UNESCO and the Academy for Educational Development. http://www.ictinedtoolkit.org/usere/library/tech_for_ed_chapters/08.pdf

Carr, D. & Lynch, B. (2006). *The International House video series.* International House.

Çelik, S., Baran, E., & Sert, O. (2018). The affordances of mobile-app supported teacher observations for peer feedback. *International Journal of Mobile and Blended Learning, 10*(2), 36–49.

Chamberlin, C. R. (2000). TESL degree candidates' perceptions of trust in supervisors. *TESOL Quarterly 34*(4), 653–672.

Chappell, P. (2014). *Group work in the English language curriculum: Sociocultural and ecological perspectives on second language classroom learning.* Springer.

Cherrington, S., & Loveridge, J. (2014). Using video to promote early childhood teachers' thinking and reflection. *Teaching and Teacher Education, 41,* 42–51.

Clara, M. (2015). What is reflection? Looking for clarity in an ambiguous notion. *Journal of Teacher Education, 66*(3), 261–271.

Clare, A. (2017). The power of video. In K. Donaghy and D. Xerri (Eds.), *The image in English language teaching* (pp. 33–42). ELT Council.

Clark, C., & Lampert, M. (1986). The study of teacher thinking: Implications for teacher education. *Journal of Teacher Education, 37*(5), 27–31.

Clarke, M. A. (1994). The dysfunctions of the theory/practice discourse. *TESOL Quarterly, 28*(1), 9–26.

Clements, P. (2015). Blog Post. *Creating a self-development record.* https://eltplanning.com/2015/05/27/reflective-practice-creating-a-self-development-record/

Cooper, R., Lavery, M., & Rinvolucri, M. (1991). *Video.* Oxford University Press.

Copland, F., Ma, G., & Mann, S. (2009). Reflecting in and on post-observation feedback in initial teacher training on certificate courses. *English Language Teacher Education and Development, 12,* 14–22.

Copland, F., Mann, S., & Graham-Marr, H. (2012). *The coursebook and beyond: Choosing, using and teaching outside the text.* Tokyo: ABAX ELT.

Copland, F., & Creese, A. (2015). *Linguistic ethnography: Collecting, analysing and presenting data.* SAGE.

Coyle, D. (2007). Content and language integrated learning: Towards a connected research agenda for CLIL pedagogies. *International Journal of Bilingual Education and Bilingualism, 10*(5), 543–562.

CraigRush, S. (2019). *Implementing a qualitative video and audio analysis study using the Transana platform: Applications for research in education settings.* SAGE.

Crasborn, F., Hennissen, P., Brouwer, N., Korthagen, F., & Bergen, T. (2011). Exploring a two-dimensional model of mentor teacher roles in mentoring dialogues. *Teaching and Teacher Education, 27*(2), 320–331.

Crichton, R., Edmett, A., & Mann, S. (2019). Video based observation and feedback for Thai in-service teachers: The mentor's role. *ELTED Journal*. https://core.ac.uk/download/pdf/225315336.pdf

Crookes, G. (2016). Educational perspectives on ELT: Society and the individual; traditional, progressive and transformative. In G. Hall (Ed.), *The Routledge handbook of English language teaching* (pp. 64–76). Routledge.

Cullen, R. (1991). Video in teacher training: The use of local materials. *English Language Teaching Journal, 45*, 33–42.

Daniil, M. (2013). *Exploring the process of reflection within teacher education: a qualitative case study of student teachers using videopapers to reflect on practice*. Doctoral dissertation, University of Bristol. https://ethos.bl.uk/OrderDetails.do?did=1&uin=uk.bl.ethos.616865

Darling-Hammond, L., & Bransford, J. D. (Eds.). (2005). *Preparing teachers for a changing world: What teachers should learn and be able to do.* Jossey-Bass.

Darling-Hammond, L., & Baratz-Snowden, J. (2007). A good teacher in every classroom: Preparing the highly qualified teachers our children deserve. *Educational Horizons, 85*(2), 111–132.

Davies, P., Perry, T., & Kirkman, J. (2017). *IRIS Connect: Developing classroom dialogue and formative feedback through collective video reflection*. Evaluation Report and Executive Summary. Education Endowment Foundation.

Dawson, P., Henderson M., Ryan, T., Mahony, P., Boud, D., Phillips, M., & Molloy, E. (2018). Technology and feedback design. In J. M. Spector, B. B. Lockee, & M. D. Childress (Eds.), *Learning, design and technology: An international compendium of theory, research, practice and policy*. Springer.

Donaghy, K. (2015). *Film in action: Teaching language using moving images*. Delta Publishing.

Donaghy, K., & Xerri, D. (2017). *The image in English language teaching*. https://www.teachingenglish.org.uk/sites/teacheng/files/The_Image_in_English_Language_Teaching.pdf

Dragas, T. (2019). Embedding reflective practice in an INSET course. In S. Walsh & S. Mann (Eds.), *The Routledge handbook of English language teacher education* (pp. 138–154). Taylor & Francis.

Driver, P. (2017). *Virtual reality and interaction design for education*. https://arro.anglia.ac.uk/id/eprint/702555/

DuFour, R., & Eaker, R. E. (1998). *Professional learning communities at work: Best practices for enhancing student achievement*. ASCD.

Edge, J. (1992). Co-operative development. *ELT Journal, 46*(1), 62–70.

Edge, J. (2011). *The reflexive teacher educator in TESOL: Roots and wings*. Routledge.

Eröz-Tuğa, B. (2013). Reflective feedback sessions using video recordings. *ELT Journal, 67*(2), 175–183.

Estapa, A., Pinnow, R. J., & Chval, K. B. (2016). Video as a professional development tool to support novice teachers as they learn to teach English language learners. *The New Educator, 12*(1), 85–104.

Ethel, R. G., & McMeniman, M. M. (2000). Unlocking the knowledge in action of an expert practitioner. *Journal of Teacher Education, 51*(2), 87–101.

Falter, M. M. & Barnes, M. E. (2020). The importance of the 'comfort zone' in preservice teachers' evaluation of video analysis sessions as a tool for enhanced reflection. *Teacher Education Quarterly, 47*(2), 64–85.

Fanselow, J. F. (1988). *Breaking rules: Generating and exploring alternatives in language teaching.* Longman.

Fanselow, J. (2018). *Small changes in teaching, Big results in learning: Videos, activities and essays to stimulate fresh thinking about language learning and teaching.* International Teacher Development Institute. https://itdi.pro/itdihome/small-changes-teaching-big-results-learning/

Fanselow, J. & Hiratsuka, T. (2019). Suggestions for teacher educators from a gentle iconoclast and a fellow explorer. In S. Walsh & S. Mann (Eds.), *The Routledge handbook of English language teacher education* (pp. 96–108). Taylor & Francis.

Farr, F. (2010). *The discourse of teaching practice feedback: A Corpus-based investigation of spoken and written modes* (Vol. 12). Routledge.

Farr, F., & Riordan, E. (2017). Prospective and practising teachers look backwards at the theory-practice divide through blogs and e-portfolios. In T. S. C. Farrell (Ed.), *TESOL voices: Insider accounts of classroom life* (pp. 13–26). TESOL Press.

Farrell, T. S. C. (2008). *Reflective language teaching: From research to practice.* Continuum.

Farrell, T. S. C. (2013). *Reflective practice in ESL teacher development groups.* Palgrave Macmillan.

Farrell, T. S. C. (2014). *Promoting teacher reflection in second language education: A framework for TESOL professionals.* Routledge.

Farrell, T. S. C. (2022). *Reflective language teaching.* Cambridge University Press.

Floman, J. L., Hagelskamp, C., Brackett, M. A., & Rivers, S. E. (2017). Emotional bias in classroom observations: within-rater positive emotion predicts favorable assessments of classroom quality. *Journal of Psychoeducational Assessment, 35*(3), 291–301.

Forest D., & Mercier A. (2011). Classroom video data and resources for teaching: Some thoughts on teacher education. In G. Gueudet, B. Pepin, & L. Trouche (Eds.), *From text to 'lived' resources.* Mathematics Teacher Education 7. Springer.

Gakonga, J. (2019). *Video use in CELTA.* ViLTE Resources. https://warwick.ac.uk/fac/soc/al/research/vilte/resources/video_use_in_celta.pdf

Gamero, M. (2017). *Dynamics of videoconferencing-mediated co-teaching in the English language classroom.* (Unpublished Masters Thesis: University of Warwick). https://warwick.ac.uk/fac/soc/al/research/vilte/resources/maricarmen_gamero_thesis.pdf

Gaudin, C., & Chaliès, S. (2015). Video viewing in teacher education and professional development: A literature review. *Educational Research Review, 16*, 41–67.

Gelfuso, A. (2016). A framework for facilitating video-mediated reflection: Supporting preservice teachers as they create 'warranted assertabilities' about literacy teaching and learning. *Teaching and Teacher Education, 58*, 68–79.

Gellevij, M., Van Der Meij, H., De Jong, T., & Pieters, J. (2002). Multimodal versus unimodal instruction in a complex learning context. *The Journal of Experimental Education, 70*(3), 215–239.

Glenn, P., & Susskind, L. (2010). How talk works: Studying negotiation interaction. *Negotiation Journal, 26*, 117–123.

Goldhammer, R. (1969). *Clinical supervision: Special methods for the supervision of teachers.* Holt, Rinehart & Winston.

Goldman, R., Pea, R., Barron, B., & Denny, S. J. (Eds.). (2007). *Video research in the learning sciences.* Erlbaum.

Goldstein, B. (2017). A history of video in ELT. *The image in English language teaching,* https://www.teachingenglish.org.uk/article/ben-goldstein-a-history-video-elt

Goldstein, B., & Driver, P. (2014). *Language learning with digital video.* Cambridge University Press.

Golombek, P. R. (2011). Dynamic assessment in teacher education: Using dialogic video protocols to intervene in teacher thinking and activity. In *Research on second language teacher education* (pp. 135–149). Routledge.

Gosling, D. (2002). *Models of peer observation of teaching.* London: LTSN Generic Centre.

Gore, J. M., & Zeichner, K. M. (1991). Action research and reflective teaching in preservice teacher education: A case study from the United States. *Teaching and Teacher Education, 7*(2), 119–136.

Graesch, A. P., Mittmann, A., Bradbury, T., & Repetti, R. (2006). Video ethnography and ethnoarchaeological tracking. In M. Pitt-Catsouphes, E. E. Kossek, & S. Sweet (Eds.), *Work and family handbook: Multi-disciplinary perspectives and approaches* (pp. 387–409). Lawrence Erlbaum.

Grossman, P., Compton, C., Igra, D., Ronfeldt, M., Shahan, E., & Williamson, P. (2009). Teaching practice: A cross-professional perspective. *Teachers College Record, 111*(9), 2055–2100.

Grushka, K., Hinde-McLeod, J., & Reynolds, R. (2005). Reflecting upon reflection: theory and practice in one Australian university teacher education program. *Reflective Practice, 6*(1), 239–246.

Gulzar, N. (2018). *Uses of electronic portfolios to foster reflective and other self-development skills in pre-service teacher education.* (Unpublished Master's Thesis. The University of Warwick, UK). Available at https://warwick.ac.uk/fac/soc/al/research/vilte/resources/gulzar_thesis.pdf

Haines, J., & Miller, P. (2016). Video-enhanced observation: Developing a flexible and effective tool. In M. O'Leary (Ed.), *Reclaiming lesson observation: Supporting excellence in teacher learning* (pp. 127–140). Routledge.

Harford, J., MacRuairc, G., & McCartan, D. (2010). 'Lights, camera, reflection': Using peer video to promote reflective dialogue among student teachers. *Teacher Development, 14*(1), 57–68.

Harmer, J. (2015). *The practice of English language teaching* (5th ed.). Pearson Longman.

Hattie, J. (2012). *Visible learning for teachers: Maximizing impact on learning.* Routledge.

Heath, C., Hindmarsh, J., & Luff, P. (2010). *Video in qualitative research.* Sage.

Hennessy, S. (2011). The role of digital artefacts on the interactive whiteboard in supporting classroom dialogue. *Journal of Computer Assisted Learning, 27*(6), 463–489.

Hennessy, S. (2014). *Bridging between research and practice: Supporting professional development through collaborative studies of classroom teaching with technology.* Sense Publishers.

Hidson, E. (2018). Video-enhanced lesson observation as a source of multiple modes of data for school leadership: A videographic approach. *Management in Education, 32*(1), 26–31.

Hiebert, J., & Hollingsworth, H. (2002). *Learning from international studies of teaching: The TIMSS-R video study.* https://research.acer.edu.au/cgi/viewcontent.cgi?referer=https://scholar.google.com/&httpsredir=1&article=1001&context=research_conference_2002

Hockly, N. (2018). Video-based observation in language teacher education. *ELT Journal, 72*(3), 329–335.

Holliday, A. (2015). Appropriate methodology: Context, culture and emergent practices. A talk given at the University of Warwick. Video available at https://warwick.ac.uk/fac/soc/al/research/groups/llta/activities/events/recorded_talks/adrian_holliday_talk/

Hottman, A. (2016). Video for all: Best practices for creating educational videos. https://warwick.ac.uk/fac/soc/al/research/vilte/resources/best-practices-for-language-education-videos.pdf

Hubber, P., White, P. & Berry, A. (2019). Using self-captured video to support reflective practice in teacher professional learning communities. In L. Xu, G. Aranda, W. Widjaja, & D. Clarke (Eds.), *Video-based research in education: Cross-disciplinary perspectives* (pp. 244–259). Routledge.

Humphries, B., & Clark, D. (2021). An examination of student preference for traditional didactic or chunking teaching strategies in an online learning environment. *Research in Learning Technology, 29.* https://doi.org/10.25304/rlt.v29.2405

Hüttner, J. (2019). Towards 'professional vision': Video as a resource in teacher learning. In S. Walsh and S. Mann (Eds.), *The Routledge handbook of English language teacher education* (pp. 473–487). Taylor & Francis.

Ipalibo-Osokolo, M. (2020). *Professional development opportunities for English language teachers in Rivers State: Affordances and constraints.* Unpublished dissertation, University of Warwick.

Jarvis, H. (2015). From PPP and CALL/MALL to a praxis of task-based teaching and mobile assisted language use. *TESL-EJ 19*(1). http://www.tesl-ej.org/wordpress/issues/volume19/ej73/ej73a1/

Jarvis, H. (2017). *TESOLacademic.org: Our ever changing story.* https://www.tesolacademic.org/msworddownloads/ELTResMarch17.pdf

Jenks, C. J., & Seedhouse, P. (2015). *International perspectives on ELT classroom interaction.* Palgrave Macmillan.

Jewitt, C. (2012). *An introduction to using video for research.* (National Centre for Research Methods Working Paper 03/12). http://eprints.ncrm.ac.uk/2259/4/NCRM_working-paper_0312.pdf

Johnson, K. E. (2009). *Second language teacher education: A sociocultural perspective.* Routledge.

Jones, S., Tanner, H., Kennewell, S., Denny, H., Anthony, C., Beauchamp, G., Jones, B., Lewis, H. & Loughran, A. (2009). Using video stimulated reflective dialogue to support the development of ICT based pedagogy in mathematics and science. *The Welsh Journal of Education, 14*(2), 63–77.

Kane, T., Gehlbach, H., Greenberg, M., Quinn, D., Thal, D. (2015). *Inviting teachers to put their 'best foot forward: Substituting teacher-collected video for in-person classroom observations.* Center for Education Policy Research, Harvard University.

Kaneko-Marques, S. M. (2015). Reflective teacher supervision through videos of classroom teaching. *Issues in Teachers' Professional Development, 17*(2), 63–79.

Kaya, M. H., & Dikilitaş, K. (2019). Constructing, reconstructing and developing teacher identity in supportive contexts. *The Asian EFL Journal, 1*(21), 58–83.

Kayaoglu, M. N. (2012). Dictating or facilitating: The supervisory process for language teachers. *Australian Journal of Teacher Education, 37*(10).

Keddie, J. (2014). *Bringing online video into the classroom.* Oxford University Press.

Kiddle, T., & Prince, T. (2019). Digital and online approaches to language teacher education. In S. Walsh and S. Mann (Eds.), *The Routledge handbook of English language teacher education* (pp. 111–124). Taylor & Francis.

Kiely, R., & Davis, M. (2010). From transmission to transformation: Teacher learning in English for speakers of other languages. *Language Teaching Research, 14*(3), 277–295.

Kilburn, D. (2014). *Methods for recording video in the classroom: Producing single and multi-camera videos for research into teaching and learning.* http://eprints.ncrm.ac.uk/3599/1/methods_for_recording_video.pdf

Kleinknecht, M., & Gröschner, A. (2016). Fostering preservice teachers' noticing with structured video feedback: Results of an online-and video-based intervention study. *Teaching and Teacher Education, 59*, 45–56.

Koc, M. (2011). Let's make a movie: Investigating pre-service teachers' reflections on using video-recorded role playing cases in Turkey. *Teaching and Teacher Education, 27*(1), 95–106.

Koc, Y., Peker, D., & Osmanoglu, A. (2009). Supporting teacher professional development through online video case study discussions: An assemblage of preservice and inservice teachers and the case teacher. *Teaching and Teacher Education, 25*(8), 1158–1168.

Körkkö, M. (2019). Towards meaningful reflection and a holistic Approach: Creating a reflection framework in teacher education. *Scandinavian Journal of Educational Research,* 1–18.

Körkkö, M., Kyrö-Ämmälä, O., & Turunen, T. (2016). Professional development through reflection in teacher education. *Teaching and Teacher Education, 55,* 198–206.

Kourieos, S. (2016). Video-mediated microteaching: A stimulus for reflection and teacher growth. *Australian Journal of Teacher Education, 41*(1), 65–80.

Kress, G. (2010). *Multimodality: A social semiotic approach to contemporary communication.* Routledge.

Kurtoglu-Hooton, N. (2010). *Post-observation feedback as an instigator of learning and change: Exploring the effect of feedback through student teachers' self-reports.* Unpublished PhD thesis, Aston University, UK.

Kurz, T. L., Llama, G., & Savenye, W. (2005). Issues and challenges of creating video cases to be used with preservice teachers. *TechTrends, 49*(4), 67–73.

Ladyshewsky, R. (2013). Instructor presence in online courses and student satisfaction. *The International Journal for the Scholarship of Teaching and Learning, 7*(1), 1–23.

Lave, J., & Wenger, E. (1991). Situated learning: Legitimate peripheral participation. Cambridge University Press.

LeBaron, C. (2008). Microethnography. In W. Dursbach (Ed.), *The international encyclopedia of communication, 7,* 3120–24. Blackwell.

Lightfoot, A. (2019). Opportunities, challenges and experiences. In S. Walsh and S. Mann (Eds.), *The Routledge handbook of English language teacher education* (pp. 52–67). Taylor & Francis.

Lindahl, K., & Baecher, L. (2016). Teacher language awareness in supervisory feedback cycles. *ELT Journal, 70*(1), 28–38.

Liu, M. H. (2016). Blending a class video blog to optimize student learning outcomes in higher education. *The Internet and Higher Education, 30,* 44–53.

Lofthouse, R., & Birmingham, P. (2010). The camera in the classroom: video-recording as a tool for professional development of student teachers. *Teacher Education Advancement Network Journal, 1*(2).

Lok, L., Schellings, G., Brouwer, N., & Den Brok, P. (2018). Investigating effects of using digital video in teacher training in Cambodia. *Journal of Technology and Teacher Education, 26*(2), 275–298.

Lonergan, J. (1984). *Video in language teaching.* Cambridge University Press.

Luna, M. J., & Sherin, M. G. (2017). Using a video club design to promote teacher attention to students' ideas in science. *Teaching and Teacher Education, 66,* 282–294.

MacKinnon, T., & Mann, S. (2016). Video as learning resource: VideoForALL project output. https://warwick.ac.uk/fac/soc/al/research/vilte/resources/video-as-a-learning-resource-for-language-teaching.pdf

Mahoney, P., Macfarlane, S., & Ajjawi, R. (2019). A qualitative synthesis of video feedback in higher education. *Teaching in Higher Education, 24*(2), 157–179.

Major, L., & Watson, S. (2018). Using video to support in-service teacher professional development: the state of the field, limitations and possibilities. *Technology, Pedagogy and Education, 27*(1), 49–68.

Mann, S., & Walsh, S. (2017). *Reflective practice in English language teaching: Research-based principles and practices.* Taylor & Francis.

Mann, S., Davidson, A., Gakonga, J., Harrison, T., Mossavian, P., & Richards, L. (2019). *Video in language teacher education.* London: British Council (ELTRA Research Report).

Mann, S., Crichton, R., & Edmett, A. (2020). Evaluating the role of video in supporting reflection beyond INSET. *System, 90,* https://doi.org/10.1016/j.system.2019.102195

Marsh, B., & Mitchell, N. (2014). The role of video in teacher professional development. *Teacher Development, 18*(3), 403–417.

Mavrou, K., Douglas, G. & Lewis, A. (2007). The use of Transana as a video analysis tool in researching computer-based collaborative learning in inclusive classrooms in Cyprus. *International Journal of Research & Method in Education, 30*(2), 163–178.

McAleavy, T., Hall-Chen, A., Horrocks, S., & Riggall, A. (2018). *Technology-supported professional development for teachers: Lessons from developing countries*. Education Development Trust.

Mercado, L., & Baecher, L. (2014). Video-based self-observation as a component of developmental teacher evaluation. *Global Education Review, 1*(3), 63–77.

Mercer, N., Hennessy, S., & Warwick, P. (2019). Dialogue, thinking together and digital technology in the classroom: Some educational implications of a continuing line of inquiry. *International Journal of Educational Research, 97*, 187–199.

Merdinger, S. (2018). *5 reasons to start audio-recording your classroom conversations, today*. Retrieved from: https://www.bakpax.com/record-classroom-conversations/

Miller, P. (2015), Video-enhanced observation: A new way to develop teacher practice. Optimus Education. http://my.optimus-education.com/video-enhanced-observation-new-way-developteacher-practice.

Miller, K., & Zhou, X. (2007). Learning from classroom video: What makes it compelling and what makes it hard. In R. Goldmann, R. Pea, B. Barron, & S. J. Derry (Eds.), *Video research in the learning sciences* (pp. 321–334). Erlbaum.

Mogallapu, A. (2011). *Social network analysis of the video bloggers' community in YouTube*. https://scholarsmine.mst.edu/cgi/viewcontent.cgi?article=5878&context=masters_theses

Moody, A. (2020). *You do for your kids: A self-study of responsible mentoring*. Unpublished doctoral dissertation, Fordham University.

Moore, C. (2015). *Learning to see, seeing to learn: The learning journey of three pre-service teachers in a video club setting*. Unpublished PhD thesis, Edith Cowan University, Australia.

Morton, T. (2019). Teacher education in content-based language education. In S. Walsh & S. Mann (Eds.), *The Routledge handbook of English language teacher education* (pp. 169–183). Taylor & Francis.

Mosley Wetzel, M., Maloch, B., & Hoffman, J. V. (2017). Retrospective video analysis: A reflective tool for teachers and teacher educators. *The Reading Teacher, 70*(5), 533–542.

Murray, D. E., & Christison, M. (2018). Online language teacher education: A review of the literature. http://aqueduto.com/wp-content/uploads/2018/12/Aqueduto-Murray-Christison.pdf

Nguyen, N. T., McFadden, A., Tangen, D., & Beutel, D. (2013). Video-stimulated recall interviews in qualitative research. In J. White (Ed.) *Proceedings of the 2013 International Conference of the Australian Association for Research in Education (AARE)*. Australian Association for Research in Education, Australia, pp. 1–10.

Nind, M., Kilburn, D., & Wiles, R. (2015). Using video and dialogue to generate pedagogic knowledge: teachers, learners and researchers reflecting together on the pedagogy of social research methods. *International Journal of Social Research Methodology, 18*(5), 561–576.

Nobre, C. (2018a). *Investigating the roles of video in teacher development*. (Unpublished Master's Thesis: University of Warwick, UK). Available at https://warwick.ac.uk/fac/soc/al/research/vilte/resources/cecilia_rodrigues_griffiths_-_ma_thesis.pdf

Nobre, V. (2018b). Mitos do Ensino do Inglês dos seus filhos [Screenshot]. YouTube. https://www.youtube.com/watch?v=XI6kweZZxSE

Olesova, L., & Borup, J. (2016). Using audio and video feedback to increase instructor presence in asynchronous online courses. In *Creating teacher immediacy in online learning environments* (pp. 235–251). IGI Global.

Ong, W. A., Swanto, S., & Alsaqqaf, A. (2020). Engaging in reflective practice via vlogs: Experience of Malaysian ESL pre-service teachers. *Linguistics, 9*, 716–724.

Pajak, E. (2003). *Honoring diverse teaching styles: A guide for supervisors.* ASCD.

Pea, R., & Lindgren, R. (2008). Video collaboratories for research and education: An analysis of collaboration design patterns. *IEEE Transactions on Learning Technologies, 1*(4), 235–247.

Peachey, N. (2015). *Digital video: A manual for language teachers.* Peachey Publications.

Phan, T. (2017). *Video recording as a tool for reflection and improving teaching practice for pre-service English language teachers.* (Unpublished MA Thesis, University of Warwick). https://warwick.ac.uk/fac/soc/al/research/vilte/resources/tran_phan_ma_thesis.pdf

Pianta, R. C., DeCoster, J., Cabell, S., Burchinal, M., Hamre, B. K., Downer, J., LoCasale-Crouch, J., Williford, A., & Howes, C. (2014). Dose–response relations between pre-school teachers' exposure to components of professional development and increases in quality of their interactions with children. *Early Childhood Research Quarterly, 29*(4), 499–508.

Prilop, C. N., Weber, K. E., & Kleinknecht, M. (2019). How digital reflection and feedback environments contribute to pre-service teachers' beliefs during a teaching practicum. *Studies in Educational Evaluation, 62,* 158–170.

Pylman, S. (2016). Reflecting on talk: A mentor teacher's gradual release in co-planning. *The New Educator, 12*(1), 48–66.

Ranellucci, J., & Bergey, B. W. (2020). Using motivation design principles to teach screencasting in online teacher education courses. *Journal of Technology and Teacher Education, 28*(2), 393–401.

Rebolledo, P., Smith, R., & Bullock, D. (Eds.). (2018). *Champion Teachers: Stories of exploratory action research.* British Council.

Rich, P. J., & Hannafin, M. (2009). Video annotation tools: Technologies to scaffold, structure, and transform teacher reflection. *Journal of Teacher Education, 60*(1), 52–67.

Roehler, L., & Cantlon, D. (1997). Scaffolding: A powerful tool in social constructivist classrooms. In K. Hogan & M. Pressley (Eds.), *Scaffolding student learning: Instructional approaches and issues* (pp. 6–42). Brookline Books.

Rosaen, C. L., Lundeberg, M., Cooper, M., Fritzen, A. & Terpstra, M. (2008). Noticing noticing: How does investigation of video records change how teachers reflect on their experiences? *Journal of Teacher Education, 59*(4), 347–360.

Rosaen, C. L., Lundeberg, M., Terpstra, M., Cooper, M., Niu, R., & Fu, J. (2010). Constructing videocases to help novices learn to facilitate discussions in science and English: How does subject matter matter? *Teachers and Teaching: Theory and Practice, 16*(4), 507–524.

Santagata, R. (2014). Towards ambitious teaching: Using video to support future teachers' reasoning about evidence of student learning. *Recherche et Formation, 75,* 95–110.

Santagata, R., & Guarino, J. (2011). Using video to teach future teachers to learn from teaching. *ZDM*, *43*(1), 133–145.

Santagata, R., & Yeh, C. (2014). Learning to teach mathematics and to analyze teaching effectiveness: Evidence from a video-and practice-based approach. *Journal of Mathematics Teacher Education*, *17*(6), 491–514.

Schepens, A., Aelterman, A., & Van Keer, H. (2007). Studying learning processes of student teachers with stimulated recall interviews through changes in interactive cognitions. *Teaching and Teacher Education*, *23*(4), 457–472.

Schön, D. A. (1983). *The reflective practitioner: How professionals think in action*. Basic Books.

Scrivener, J. (2011). *Learning teaching* (3rd ed.). Macmillan Education.

Scrivener, J. (2012). *Classroom management techniques*. Cambridge University Press.

Seedhouse, P. (Ed.). (2021). *Video enhanced observation for language teaching: Reflection and professional development*. Bloomsbury.

Sert, O. (2010). A proposal for a CA-integrated English language teacher education program in Turkey. *Asian EFL Journal* (Special Issue on English Language Teacher Education and Development: Issues and Perspectives in Asia, ed. Eva Bernat), *12*(3), 62 97.

Sert, O. (2013). Integrating digital video analysis software into language teacher education: Insights from conversation analysis. *Procedia – Social and Behavioral Sciences*, *70*, 231 238.

Sert, O. (2015). *Social interaction and L2 classroom discourse*. Edinburgh University Press.

Sert, O. (2019). Classroom interaction and language teacher education. In S. Walsh and S. Mann (Eds.), *The Routledge handbook of English language teacher education* (pp. 216–238). Taylor & Francis.

Sert, O. (2020). Transforming CA findings into future L2 teaching practices: Challenges and prospects for teacher education. In S. Kunitz, N. Markee, & O. Sert (Eds.), *Classroom-based conversation analytic research: Theoretical and applied perspectives on pedagogy* (pp. 259–280). Springer.

Sherin, M. G. (2007). The development of teachers' professional vision in video clubs. In R. Goldman, R. Pea, B. Barron, & S. Derry (Eds.), *Video research in the learning sciences* (pp. 383–395). Routledge.

Sherin, M. G., & Han, S. Y. (2004). Teacher learning in the context of a video club. *Teaching and Teacher Education*, *20*, 163–183.

Sherin, M., & van Es, E. A. (2009). Effects of video club participation on teachers' professional vision. *Journal of Teacher Education*, *60*(1), 20–37.

Sherman, J. (2003). *Using authentic video in the classroom*. Cambridge University Press.

Sitzmann, T., Ely, K., Brown, K. G., and Bauer, K. N. (2010). Self-assessment of knowledge: A cognitive learning or affective measure? *Academy of Management Learning & Education*, *9*(2), 169–191.

Smith, M. G. (2019). A video-mediated critical friendship reflection framework for ESL teacher education. *TESL-EJ*, *23*(1).

Snelson, C., & Hsu, Y. C. (2019). Educational 360-degree videos in virtual reality: A scoping review of the emerging research. *TechTrends*, 1–9.

Stannard, R., & Mann S. (2018). Using screen capture feedback to establish social presence and increase student engagement: A genuine innovation in feedback. In C. H. Xiang (Ed.) *Cases on audio-visual media in language education* (pp. 93–117). IGI Global.

Stannard, R., & Sallı, A. (2019). Using screen capture technology in teacher education. In S. Walsh & S. Mann (Eds.), *The Routledge handbook of English language teacher education* (pp. 459–472). Taylor & Francis.

Star, J. R., & Strickland, S. K. (2008). Learning to observe: Using video to improve preservice mathematics teachers' ability to notice. *Journal of mathematics teacher education, 11*(2), 107–125.

Stempleski, S., & Tomalin, B. (2001). *Film.* Oxford University Press.

Sterrett, W., Dikkers, A. G., & Parker, M. (2014). Using brief instructional video clips to foster communication, reflection, and collaboration in schools. *The Educational Forum 78*(3), 263–274.

Stigler, J. W., Gallimore, R., & Hiebert, J. (2000). Using video surveys to compare classrooms and teaching across cultures: Examples and lessons from the TIMSS video studies. *Educational Psychologist, 35*(2), 87–100.

Stockero, S. L. (2008). Using a video-based curriculum to develop a reflective stance in prospective mathematics teachers. *Journal of Mathematics Teacher Education, 11*(5), 373–394.

Stokes, L. R., Suh, J. M., & Curby, T. W. (2020). Examining the nature of teacher support during different iterations and modalities of lesson study implementation. *Professional Development in Education, 46*(1), 97–111.

Streeck, J., & Mehus, S. (2005). Microethnography: The study of practices. *Handbook of language and social interaction*, K. L. Fitch and R. E. Sanders (Eds.), 381–406, Lawrence Erlbaum.

Sydnor, J. (2016). Using video to enhance reflective practice: Student teachers' dialogic examination of their own teaching. *The New Educator, 12*(1), 67–84.

Tan, A. L., & Towndrow, P. A. (2009). Catalyzing student–teacher interactions and teacher learning in science practical formative assessment with digital video technology. *Teaching and Teacher Education, 25*(1), 61–67.

Taqwa, A. & Sandi, V. N. (2019). Students' experiences of using vlogs to learn English. *Journal of Foreign Language Teaching and Learning, 4*(1), 1–13.

Tardy, C. M. & Snyder, B. (2004). 'That's Why I Do It': Flow and EFL teachers' practices'. *ELT Journal, 58*, 118–128.

Thaler, E. (2012). *Englisch unterrichten: Grundlagen, kompetenzen, methoden.* Cornelsen.

Thompson, J., & Kosiorek, C. (2017). *A quick guide to video coaching: The best practice to improve the art and craft of teaching through guided reflection.* Kindle Edition available at https://www.amazon.com/Quick-Guide-Video-Coaching-reflection/dp/0692996672

Thompson, R., & Lee, M. J. (2012). Talking with students through screencasting: Experimentations with video feedback to improve student learning. *The Journal of Interactive Technology and Pedagogy, 1*(1), 1–16.

Toci, V., Camizzi, L., Goracci, S., Borgi, R., De Santis, F., Coscia, L., Perrone, F., Cigognini, M., & Pettenati, M. (2015). Designing, producing and exemplifying videos to support reflection and metacognition for in-service teachers training. *Journal of e-Learning and Knowledge Society, 11*(2). https://www.learntechlib.org/p/151059/

Tripp, T. R., & Rich, P. J. (2012). The influence of video analysis on the process of teacher change. *Teaching and Teacher Education, 28*(5), 728–739.

Tsui, A. B. (2009). Distinctive qualities of expert teachers. *Teachers and Teaching: Theory and Practice, 15*(4), 421–439.

Urmeneta, C. E., & Walsh, S. (2017). Classroom interactional competence in content and language integrated learning. *Applied Linguistics Perspectives on CLIL, 1*, 183 200.

Vásquez, C., & Reppen, R. (2007). Transforming practice: Changing patterns of participation in post-observation meetings. *Language Awareness, 16*(3), 153–172.

VEO Europa. (2017, October 2). *Veo Europa Project*. VEO Europa Project. Retrieved February 12, 2022, from https://veoeuropa.com/

Verlaan, W., & Verlaan, S. (2015). Using video-reflection with pre-service teachers: A cautionary tale. In E. Ortlieb, M. McVee, & L. Shanahan (Eds.), *Video reflection in literacy teacher education and development* (Vol. 5, pp. 151–171). Emerald Group.

ViLTE. *Video in Language Teacher Education.* (2019). University of Warwick. https://warwick.ac.uk/fac/soc/al/research/vilte/

Villacañas de Castro, L. S. (2020). Translating teacher funds of identity into curricular proposals for the EFL classroom: A model for student-teacher innovation and professional development. *Journal of Language, Identity & Education, 19*(1), 25–41.

Wallace, M. J., & Bau, T. H. (1991). *Training foreign language teachers: A reflective approach.* Cambridge University Press.

Walsh, S. (2006). *Investigating classroom discourse.* Routledge.

Walsh, S. (2011). *Exploring classroom discourse: Language in action.* Routledge.

Walsh, S. (2013). *Classroom discourse and teacher development.* Edinburgh University Press.

Walsh, S. (2018). SETTVEO: Evidence-based reflection and teacher development. *Teaching English ELT Research Papers, 19*, 1–24.

Walsh, S. (2020). *Evidence-based reflection and teacher development.* British Council Research Report. https://www.teachingenglish.org.uk/article/evidence-based-reflection-teacher-development

Walsh, S., & Mann, S. (2015). Doing reflective practice: A data-led way forward. *ELT Journal 69*(4), 351–362.

Walshe, N., & Driver, P. (2019). Developing reflective trainee teacher practice with 360-degree video. *Teaching and Teacher Education, 78*, 97–105.

Ward, J. R., & McCotter, S. S. (2004). Reflection as a visible outcome for preservice teachers. *Teaching and Teacher Education, 20*(3), 243–257.

Waring, H. Z. (2013). Two mentor practices that generate teacher reflection without explicit solicitations: Some preliminary considerations. *RELC Journal, 44*(1), 103–119.

Webb, K. (2020). *Peer observation for development: If you don't have the right ingredients, you can't cook the dish.* ELTED, 23, 48–60.

Weber, K. E., Gold, B., Prilop, C. N. & Kleinknecht, M. (2018). Promoting pre-service teachers' professional vision of classroom management during practical school training:

Effects of a structured online-and video-based self-reflection and feedback intervention. *Teaching and Teacher Education, 76*, 39–49.

Whitcher, A. (2017). Image makers: the new language learners of the 21st century. In K. Donaghy and D. Xerri, (Eds.), *The image in English language teaching* (pp. 13–22). ELT Council: Malta.

Whitcomb, J., Borko, H., & Liston, D. (2009). Growing talent: Promising professional development models and practices. *Journal of Teacher Education, 60*(3), 207–212.

Whyte, S., & Schmid, E. C. (2018). Classroom technology for young learners. In S. Garton and F. Copland (Eds.), *The Routledge handbook of teaching English to young learners* (pp. 338–355). Routledge.

Windscheid, J., & Will, A. (2018). *A web-based multi-screen 360-degree video player for pre-service teacher training.* Universitätsbibliothek.

Woods, P. (1993). Critical events in education. *British Journal of Sociology of Education, 14,* 355–371.

Xu, L., Aranda, G., Widjaja, W., & Clarke, D. (Eds.). (2018). *Video-based research in education: Cross-disciplinary perspectives.* Routledge.

Yeh, C., & Santagata, R. (2015). Pre-Service Teachers' Learning to Generate Evidence-Based Hypotheses about the Impact of Mathematics Teaching on Learning. *Journal of Teacher Education, 66*(1), 21–34.

Yuan, R., Mak, P., & Yang, M. (2020). 'We teach, we record, we edit, and we reflect': Engaging pre-service language teachers in video-based reflective practice. *Language Teaching Research*, https://doi.org/10.1177/1362168820906281

Zeichner, K. (2010). Rethinking the connections between campus courses and field experiences in college-and university-based teacher education. *Journal of Teacher Education, 61*(1–2), 89–99.

Zhang, M., Lundeberg, M., Koehler, M. J., & Eberhardt, J. (2011). Understanding affordances and challenges of three types of video for teacher professional development. *Teaching and Teacher Education, 27*(2), 454–462.

Index

action research 42, 130–3, 136, 151, 155
animation 44, 45
annotation 8, 19, 20, 41, 72–4, 76, 78,
 136, 137, 146, 156
anxiety 110
apps 8, 10, 11, 30
appraisal 89, 96, 109, 115, 124, 127
approach
 competency-based approach 26
 constructivist approach/ constructivism
  18, 22–3
 inductive approach 105
 transmission approach 18
artefacts 10, 38, 42, 53, 60, 62, 68, 80, 86,
 96, 115, 118, 123, 130, 137, 151
assessment 12–13, 29–31, 46, 62, 82,
 107–10, 114, 119
autonomy 3, 7, 42
awareness 3, 14, 20, 24, 27, 30, 36, 41, 50,
 68, 74–7, 125, 129

benchmarking 28
bias 59, 62, 64–5, 126
blended learning 5, 16, 18

camera 2, 14–15, 40, 44, 113, 125, 131,
 134, 136
captioning 4, 69, 72
checklist 52, 53, 65, 93, 102, 108–9

classroom
 mapping 61, 79
 practice 2, 19, 25, 28, 31, 37, 48, 50, 58,
  62, 80–1, 109, 121, 137
classroom language
 clarification request 20, 72
 display question 20, 72
 echo 20, 72
 elicitation 72, 100, 105
 feedback 4, 13–14, 26, 28–9, 31–3,
  36, 39, 42, 47–8, 50, 52, 60, 69, 72,
  84, 86, 89, 92, 96, 98–100, 104, 106,
  110
 gesture 6, 9, 17, 115
coaching 16, 128
comment 35, 73, 120, 132, 139
consent 12, 96
critical incident 86, 90

data collection 102, 129–32
description (reflective levels) 14, 96, 108
dialogic reflection 20, 22, 80
distance learning 16, 18, 47, 113, 115

editing 1, 3–4, 9, 26–7, 43, 45–6, 72, 131,
 138
e-portfolio 37, 74
evaluation
 peer-evaluation 16, 74

Facebook 42
facilitation/facilitator 8, 10, 67, 80, 96,
    101–3, 117–118
flipped learning/training 3, 32, 47

instructional rounds 103
Interaction 5, 7–8, 10, 14, 18, 20, 32, 53,
    62, 66–8, 72–5, 79–80, 82, 84–6, 91,
    98, 103, 105, 113, 117, 127, 129–32

language 4, 6
language teacher 6–9, 12, 14–15, 17–18,
    21, 26, 33, 54, 58, 66, 137
learning community 39
learner 7, 9, 14, 20, 27, 32, 44, 64, 66, 81,
    97, 126
length 33, 49–51, 54, 57, 70–1, 80, 89, 101
lesson observation 21, 32, 111
lesson plan 84, 104, 116–118, 120, 124
lesson study 29, 103, 104
logistics 105, 124

mediating/mediation 23, 60–1, 63, 79,
    81, 128
meta-analysis 18, 21
methodology 3, 9, 22, 25–6, 31, 35, 131,
    133
mentor/ mentoring 24, 37, 43, 107–8,
    110, 133
micro ethnography 61, 86, 106
microteaching 18, 24, 29, 37, 85
multimodality 6, 7, 130

note taking 68–9
noticing 3, 7, 20, 23, 36, 49, 51, 59, 62,
    67–8, 71, 74, 81, 109, 111–112, 115,
    121–2, 126

observation
    in-person observation 113
    pre-observation 106, 116
    sight observation 105
    sound observation 105
    video-based observation 31–2, 95, 105,
        112–113, 131

peer observation 3, 29, 77, 95–6, 98, 102–
    6, 109, 111, 127
peer reflection 24, 94
post-observation conference (POC) 112–
    113, 119, 125
practicum 23, 27, 29–30, 90–1, 115
praxis 35–6
privacy 40, 96
professional development 16–17, 19, 21–
    3, 37, 39, 47, 50, 54, 76, 85–6, 98,
    107, 111, 122, 137
protocol 55, 63, 102, 105, 114, 123–4, 127

recording 12, 17, 32, 35, 41, 44–5, 47, 66–
    7, 75, 77, 84–5, 93, 96, 99, 105, 116,
    120, 124, 127, 129, 131–2, 134–5
reflection
    teacher reflection 17, 79–82, 121
    reflection-for-action 60–1
    reflection-in-action 60–1, 134
    reflection-on-action 60–1, 69
reflective practice (RP) 6, 20, 24, 29, 33,
    60, 74, 94, 97, 99, 123, 130
research 15–16, 18–21, 25, 27, 33, 39–
    40, 42, 47, 66, 72, 75, 77, 87, 94, 102,
    112, 120, 126

screencasting 16, 38, 47–8
self-assessment 29, 46, 62, 107–9, 119
self-development 82, 87
self-observation 30, 32, 76, 79, 81–3, 85–
    6, 89, 91, 93, 106–7, 109, 114, 124–5
self-reflection 28, 67, 91–2, 119, 121–3,
    132
stimulated recall 16, 33, 120, 129, 132–5
storage 19, 120
student
    student/learner 13, 17–18, 21, 23–4,
        26–8, 34, 49
    student-centred teaching 17, 117

student talk 50, 60, 66, 107
supervision/supervisor 110–119, 121–2, 125, 127

tagging 20, 61, 72–3, 75–6, 78, 119–20
talk 8, 17–18, 20, 29–30, 39, 42, 50, 52, 60, 66–7, 70, 74–5, 81, 85–7, 98, 100, 106–7, 112
tallying 61, 71, 79, 85
task 9–10, 25–6, 33, 52–3, 63–4, 66, 69–71, 76, 84, 87, 90
teacher
    INSET teacher/in-service 21–2, 107
    novice teacher 24, 36, 81, 84
    PRESET teacher/pre-service 22, 24, 26–7, 29, 110
    Teacher Activity Groups (TAG) 100
    teacher development 14, 16, 22, 38, 54, 77, 100
teacher educator 27, 42–3, 47–8, 50, 60, 62, 73
teacher learning 6–8, 14, 19, 21, 23, 35, 37–8, 48–9, 54, 59, 66, 93, 100, 106, 110, 116, 121–2, 127
    teacher talk 20, 30, 66, 75, 107, 112, 119–20, 122, 125
    teacher training 16, 18, 21, 22, 35, 55, 91
teams 32, 38, 40, 41
TikTok 42–3
timestamping 72, 74, 76
trainee 29, 33, 39, 50, 57, 77, 81, 115
transcript/ transcription 67, 85, 126, 138

video
    demo video 107

digital video 7, 10, 17, 23, 58, 72, 129
live video 39
video analysis 17, 19, 21, 30, 34, 37, 53–4, 59, 63, 74, 81–2, 86, 97, 102, 110, 118, 123, 127–8
video case 15, 50
video clip 109
video club model 101
videoconference 41, 45, 114
video content 9, 11, 12, 15, 25, 54
video-enhanced observation (VEO) 16, 20, 74–8, 98–9, 110, 119–20
video format 42
video library 54
video production 42, 44, 47–8
video recording 17, 75, 93, 116, 120, 124, 127, 134
video review 68, 79, 81, 86, 95, 108–12, 116, 128, 130
vignette 12, 14, 31, 35, 39–41, 51, 53, 74–5, 90–1, 98–9, 115, 118, 134
ViLTE 15, 17, 25, 30–1, 42, 50, 58, 84–5, 99, 136
Vimeo 11, 27, 42, 47, 53
virtual learning environment (VLE) 32, 47
virtual reality (VR) 16, 136
vlog 42–3, 131

wait time 34, 72, 81, 89, 105, 108, 127
WhatsApp 33, 40

YouTube 11, 32, 42–3, 47, 53, 67, 69, 73, 137

Zoom 15–16, 32, 38, 41, 45, 113

CPSIA information can be obtained
at www.ICGtesting.com
Printed in the USA
JSHW011207270623
43765JS00001B/9

9 781781 797556